Routledge Revivals

Euripides and Shaw

Euripides and Shaw (1921) looks at Bernard Shaw and English Drama as great stylistic changes were sweeping the English stage. Shaw and Euripides are compared, and the important plays of the time are examined before moving on to an analysis of the very facets of drama itself.

Euripides and Shaw

With Other Essays

Gilbert Norwood

First published in 1921
by Methuen & Co. Ltd.

This edition first published in 2025 by Routledge
4 Park Square, Milton Park, Abingdon, Oxon, OX14 4RN

and by Routledge
605 Third Avenue, New York, NY 10017

Routledge is an imprint of the Taylor & Francis Group, an informa business

© 1921 Methuen & Co. Ltd.

All rights reserved. No part of this book may be reprinted or reproduced or utilised in any form or by any electronic, mechanical, or other means, now known or hereafter invented, including photocopying and recording, or in any information storage or retrieval system, without permission in writing from the publishers.

Publisher's Note
The publisher has gone to great lengths to ensure the quality of this reprint but points out that some imperfections in the original copies may be apparent.

Disclaimer
The publisher has made every effort to trace copyright holders and welcomes correspondence from those they have been unable to contact.

A Library of Congress record exists under LCCN: 22005407

ISBN: 978-1-032-95527-8 (hbk)
ISBN: 978-1-003-58532-9 (ebk)
ISBN: 978-1-032-95530-8 (pbk)

Book DOI 10.4324/9781003585329

EURIPIDES AND SHAW

WITH OTHER ESSAYS

BY

GILBERT NORWOOD

METHUEN & CO. LTD.
36 ESSEX STREET W.C.
LONDON

First Published in 1921

NOTE

TWO of these essays were originally lectures. "Euripides and Shaw" was delivered in 1911, "The Present Renaissance of English Drama" in 1913. I have to thank the Literary and Debating Society of Newport (Mon.) and the Editor of the *Welsh Outlook* respectively for permission to reprint them. Both have been revised, and the second has been brought up to date.

For the Index I am indebted to the kindness of my friend, Mr. Cyril Brett.

GILBERT NORWOOD

PRESTON

CONTENTS

	PAGE
EURIPIDES AND SHAW: A COMPARISON	1
THE PRESENT RENAISSANCE OF ENGLISH DRAMA	49
THE NATURE AND METHODS OF DRAMA	109
INDEX	211

EURIPIDES AND SHAW

A COMPARISON

OUR subject can best be understood if viewed, in the first instance, historically. Both Euripides and Mr. Bernard Shaw have been voices of an age of reaction, of an age which stood in marked and recognized contrast to the era which had immediately preceded it. Let us begin then with the briefest historical survey and endeavour to compare these two reactions.

It is usually hard or impossible for any man to describe, perhaps even to understand, the history and spirit of his own generation. But the present epoch is exceptional; it can be understood even by those who live in it if they keep before their eyes a strong contrast, precisely the contrast which it is my present business to indicate. There is a real gulf between us and the middle of the nineteenth century. In England, at any rate, the march of affairs broke into a kind of hand-gallop, ending with a leap over a chasm which can hardly be defined, into a morass from which we have not yet found our way. This jerk in our progress, this turning-point (to use a more decorous metaphor), is to be found in the Education Act of 1870, a piece of legislation which has already given results of gigantic importance, generating and letting loose energies, the history of which has hardly more than begun. But their activity has already shaken society. On many momentous subjects it is impossible for us to think or act as we thought and acted fifty years ago. The present age is severed from what is called the Victorian era with a completeness which is truly amazing when we consider the fewness of the years; but not more amazing than the extent to which analogous conditions enable us to enter into the spirit of an epoch so far sundered from us in time as the age of Euripides. We can understand Pericles better than we understand Palmerston.

It will be enough for our purpose if we confine ourselves to pointing out the difference in spirit between the present time and the Victorian age. Consider the legislation of two generations ago, the tone and the implied assumptions of statesmen, of orators, of political and social theorists; the formulæ, sometimes not expressed but often definitely proclaimed, which ruled the different classes of society in their inward life and their outward contacts. Above all, consider the literature of those days—the writers who were not only great but also popular, and who therefore voiced the opinions and emotions of their less articulate fellows —Dickens, Macaulay, Wordsworth, Tennyson. Add to these that invaluable chronicle of manners and customs, the back numbers of *Punch*. Are we not already far enough removed from them to observe, in spite of their manifold differences, a unity of spirit, a definite tone? Above all we are conscious of a robust faith in everything English and of the nineteenth century, a certainty that all the men of the past have been but so many coral insects building up that perfect structure which has at last emerged above the waters of humiliation and experiment into the sunshine of the Great Exhibition. England is the heir of all the ages and the centre of space. From London there is a slight fall to the provinces, and then again to Scotland and Wales, with a deep but isolated depression to mark Ireland. The level falls rapidly as we come to "foreigners," among whom the French have a bad pre-eminence. Farther down the slope are Germans, Americans, and then the rest of Europe. Thus at length we reach the dim collections of humanity known as "natives," whose territory provides the Englishman with a species of drill-hall in which to exercise his celebrated bull-dog virtues and enjoy to the full the luxury of patronizing people who can never annoy him by rivalry.

Even the greatest of the popular writers were not untainted by this childishness. The more free an author was from it, the harder was it for him to gain a high reputation in his own day; Carlyle is an example, and Shelley above all. In the work of those who really struck the imagination of their contemporaries, in writers like Macaulay and Tennyson, there is a tone of gentlemanly arrogance, of urbane self-satisfaction, which impels one to echo Sydney Smith's wistful remark: "I wish I were as sure of anything as Tom Macaulay is of everything."

Since those days we have passed through a profound reaction. The nation which seemed to believe that Queen Victoria was immortal has seen her fade into a name to which there clings already the faintest strange tinge of unfamiliarity. With that great figure has departed all the crude but not ignoble certainty, all the superficial worship of progress. The heir of all the ages has cut the entail. Where most we were self-confident, we question most. We who spoke with such confidence about far Cathay have begun to realize how little we know of our own country. The people that saw a great light now sits in darkness, half-lit by gleams of which it knows not whether they are the radiance of a new dawn or the marsh-fires of diseased yearning and perverted energy.

It would be an almost warrantable conciseness to remark at this point that, as for the reaction in which Euripides was a leading figure, it has been already described; that the contrast between the period of his greatest activity—or, to put it more accurately, of his extant dramas—and the earlier part of the fifth century B.C. is roughly the same as the contrast in England. The magnificent exploits of Athens in the struggle against Persia, the political power and the undying glory which she had won by her victories over the barbarian invaders, had indeed given an enormous impulse to Athenian patriotism and so to the national art in its varied forms of the drama, painting, sculpture, and architecture, an impulse reminding us of the flood of pride and energy which filled the English nation during and after its contest with Napoleon. But by the time at which the Peloponnesian War broke out (the year 431 B.C.), which is also, roughly, the time of Euripides' earliest surviving work, this impulse had already passed away. Athens had begun to descend from the pinnacle of political and artistic achievement. She was, indeed, destined still to be important in politics, and her literature, both in poetry and in prose, maintained itself at a splendid height, but for the time decadence seemed to have set its mark everywhere else. The Delian League had become an empire and then a tyranny; philosophy was for a while, to all appearance, undermined by the shallow accomplishments of the Sophists; democracy was decoming ochlocracy. The spectacle of the rapid fading of so much glory had tainteb men with that cynicism of which Euripides often speaks. Like Shaw, he was compelled by the urgency of his environment and by the law of his own nature to express the prevalent sense of moral and intellectual bankruptcy, but at the same moment to seek for, and to follow, the road towards a new, more humble, hope.

Let so much suffice as an outline of the historical conditions which have brought these two great dramatists into a kinship of ideas and method. It is now time that we should study this similarity in a more detailed manner. The comparison between Euripides and Mr. Shaw has often been made and is, indeed, quaintly suggested to us by the delightful passage in *Major Barbara* where Shaw himself alludes to Euripides, and almost brings him upon his stage in the person of the professor of Greek. There are four main features which are to be found in both dramatists, characteristics of fundamental importance in the workmanship and intellectual outlook of both.

First should be placed a spirit of challenge to all accepted beliefs. The dramatist sees around him a whole world of assumptions, a whole gallery of revered portraits of human greatness. He is the very voice of an age of questions, and by the law of his nature he insists on revising all notions however fundamental, all conventions however universal, all religious systems however august. This by no means implies that he thinks the whole world mistaken. He may, perhaps, endorse the verdict of ages when he has completed his examination—but not before. He feels that the world spurns all truth while it is fresh and stimulating, embracing it only when, by the force of obsolescence, it is already becoming error. Once in every generation at least, a nation must take stock of its creed and its conduct. The whole history of human sorrow and waste is nothing but the admission that such revisions have been often and terribly overdue.

It is the deep glory of these two writers that their self-examination, their sturdy singularity, their almost fierce determination to sound and test everything, is as complete as it can be in a human creature. This merciless sincerity can endure the last trial of all: they are both capable of ridiculing their own reasoned position as if it were the most superficial pose. Take this passage from *The Doctor's Dilemma*. It occurs in the scene where Louis Dubedat, artistically a genius but morally a complete scoundrel, is confronted by a sort of committee of doctors, who are trying to bring his baseness home to him:

LOUIS: You're on the wrong tack altogether. I'm not a criminal. All your moralizings have no value for me. I don't believe in morality. I'm a disciple of Bernard Shaw.
SIR PATRICK: Bernard Shaw? I never heard of him. He's a Methodist preacher, I suppose?
LOUIS (*scandalized*): No, no. He's the most advanced man now living: he isn't anything.

What could be more clear than that Mr. Shaw, under the flippancy of this, is quite aware how his own position about morality —a position he has elsewhere succinctly defined in the words " morality may go to its father the Devil "—may become a mere pose and a justification for any clever blackguard? He is always turning on his own would-be followers. The whole of that slight amusing piece called *How He Lied to her Husband* is an example—a demonstration of what cheap folly even such a profoundly touching and indeed terrible situation as that of *Candida* may become when transplanted to an atmosphere of secondhand characters and shoddy thinking.

Turn for a moment to Euripides, and we find a surprisingly similar case in the *Bacchæ*, his last and perhaps his greatest drama. Throughout his life Euripides has been attacking the traditional beliefs about the orthodox Olympian gods with every resource of his splendid moral earnestness, his intellectual penetration, and his technical skill. And yet, at the end of his life, what does he say?

I do not rationalize about the gods. Those ancestral traditions, coeval with time, which are our possession, no reason can overthrow, not even if subtle brains have discovered what they call wisdom.

This passage, which I have translated clumsily but as fairly as I can, has often been regarded as the poet's recantation of the convictions and the teaching of a lifetime. I, for one, cannot think so. It is unsafe to affirm anything more definite than this, that the poet is setting himself against dilettantism in matters where dilettantism is fatal. A restless spirit of inquiry into the credentials of traditional ideas, on whatever

A COMPARISON

subject, had long been general in the more cultivated communities of Greece. Nothing, however venerable, could escape a close and often hostile scrutiny. In this movement Euripides had taken a leading part, and he was just as ready in his latest years—this the *Bacchæ*, as a whole, abundantly proves—to fight for the same cause as he had been when young. But he was at odds with those who made a potent medicine their daily beverage—those young wits of whom Aristophanes says that " the give-me-a-definition look is coming out on you for all the world like a rash." Euripides had found that it was as important to restrain, even to disown, disciples who made his principles an excuse for their own folly and misbehaviour, as to insist on the principles themselves.

But this is only a special case, striking though it may be as the final proof of spiritual clearness and candour; both these writers know practically no limits to their range of scrutiny. Think of the number of typical heroes whom Mr. Shaw turns inside out—the different kinds of men and women who have been, and, are, revered as pillars of society and stalwart witnesses to the greatness of humanity. Sergius Saranoff, the splendid warrior who turns defeat into victory by a heroic cavalry-charge, and comes home to the plaudits of his friends and the rapturous homage of his future bride —how he wilts in the cold dry air of Shavian criticism! His cavalry-charge is an insane act of suicide which succeeds by miracle because the enemy run short of ammunition; his love affair is an elaborate pose of courtly adoration on both sides; his melodramatic affectations are punctured at every turn by the irony of circumstances or by the contrast of the real humdrum value of the Swiss officer whom he despises.

Candida—an even finer play than *Arms and the Man*—contains a similar example of this method. There the character to be vivisected like Sergius is Morell the clergyman. The searchlight is turned pitilessly upon his weakness and self-indulgence, but —this is a point of vast importance—he is not the ordinary clergyman of theatrical satire. He is neither the inept fool of *The Private Secretary* nor the farcical sham-ecclesiastic of *The Importance of Being Earnest*. He is a good Christian, hard-working and sympathetic, a fine speaker, an intelligent thorough man, a man even with some sense of humour. We see through him in the end, but it is asuredly not because we find his goodness to be a fraud, his sympathy a piece of professional technique. Morell is no hypocrite grinding his teeth in the last act; he will preach just as well and sincerely to-morrow — nay, with greater sincerity and effect. He is found out simply because Mr. Shaw is keen-sighted enough to disregard conventional reverence for the popular clergyman and to see and show us the human being underneath. Morell is as good as most people, but he is not so much better as we thought and as he thought. He has mistaken bustle for life, applause for conversion; we all do this. The dramatist has turned aside from such easy quarry as the forger, the child-stealer, the betrayer of political secrets, and all the rest of popular villains; he has studied ordinary people.

If his work at any point impinges upon melodrama, it is only that he may the more startlingly convince us of the truth by its contrast with theatrical absurdity. Shaw begins where melodrama leaves off. Most of us have, in the presence of a child, told some laughable anecdote which ends abruptly with a repartee, whereupon the child has asked, "And what did the other man say?" Shaw is for ever telling us what the other man says and does; often it is the best part of the story. General Burgoyne, in *The Devil's Disciple*, is describing to his colleague the plight of his forces when face to face with the American insurgents :—

Do you at all realize, sir, that we have nothing standing between us and destruction but our own bluff and the sheepishness of these colonists? They are men of the same English stock as ourselves: six to one of us, six to one, sir; and nearly half our troops are Hessians, Brunswickers, German dragoons, and Indians with scalping-knives. These are the countrymen on whose devotion you rely! Suppose the colonists find a leader! Suppose the news from Springtown should turn out to mean that they have already found a leader! What shall we do then, eh?

Now comes the crushing answer of the footlights :—

Our duty, sir, I presume.

Loud cheers and a Union Jack in the

background, with quick curtain? No. Burgoyne is allowed to reply :—

Quite so, quite so. Thank you, Major Swindon, thank you. Now you've settled the question, sir—thrown a flood of light on the situation. What a comfort to me to feel that I have at my side so devoted and able an officer to support me in this emergency! I think, sir, it will probably relieve both our feelings if we proceed to hang this dissenter without further delay, especially as I am debarred by my principles from the customary military vent for my feelings.

Or take a simpler example from *The Man of Destiny*. Napoleon is addressing a woman who has robbed one of his officers of some papers :—

NAPOLEON: I am waiting for the despatches. I shall take them, if necessary, with as little ceremony as the handkerchief.
THE LADY: General, do you threaten women?
NAPOLEON: Yes.

Is this merely a theatrical trick, the knowledge when, and when not, to drop the curtain? Assuredly not. One of Mr. Shaw's constant aims is to free his hearers from the dominion of mere phrases. The power of these catchwords consists in this, that they impress the surface of the mind with a sense of dignity, above all of finality. Therefore the surest way to break the spell is to refuse to regard them as final, to consider them open to question; and, in the drama, to allow an opportunity of reply. At the same time as he clears away this verbal lumber, Mr. Shaw throws off allegiance to the conventional hero, the pillar of society, the demigod of the stage. His plays are full of these discredited pundits: Sir Ralph Bloomfield Bonnington, the great physician; Mrs. Dudgeon, the godly mater-familias; Napoleon, the Man of Destiny: Broadbent, the liberal-minded Englishman; Sir Howard Hallam, the upright judge; Morell once more, and Major Saranoff.

Euripides will be found to supply a list equally long and significant. First let us look at Achilles in the *Iphigenia at Aulis*, a character not unlike Sergius Saranoff. This dazzling Homeric hero, the most glorious figure in Greek story, finds himself here in an awkward and ludicrous situation. The Greek host has assembled at Aulis, about to cross the sea to Troy under the leadership of Agamemnon. But contrary winds have been sent by the goddess Artemis; the leaders are in despair, the army on the verge of mutiny. At this point the prophet Calchas informs Agamemnon that the wrath of Artemis can be averted only if Agamemnon will sacrifice Iphigenia, his own daughter; on the altar of the goddess. After much wretched hesitation the King consents and summons her from her home in Argos. The hideous purpose of her coming is concealed; Agamemnon sends a message that he wishes to marry her to Achilles, the son of the goddess Thetis. But he tells Achilles nothing of this plot. In due time the maiden arrives, but her father learns with horror that her mother, his wife, has shared her journey. Not only is his heart breaking at the coming slaughter; he knows that he will have to face his wife's desperate opposition. For the moment he contrives to withdraw, but in his absence Clytæmnestra and her daughter learn from an old slave the true meaning of the summons. They decide to appeal to Achilles, and when he comes upon the scene Clytæmnestra makes a desperate yet dignified appeal. What is his reply? He is represented by all tradition as the son of a goddess, by far the bravest and strongest of the Greek warriors; in Homer the very sound of his battle-cry is enough to make the Trojans flee. How does he act now? Does he bestow three or four lines of hurried consolation on the distressed ladies and then, brandishing his sword, bound away to hew Agamemnon and his followers into a more reasonable frame of mind, after which, no doubt, he returns to marry Iphigenia in sober earnest? No. He makes a speech which it is worth while to quote at length, for its length is important. And we must remember that all the while a royal lady is hanging upon his words in unspeakable anguish. Thus then Achilles:—

Magnanimously my heart is lifted on high; it knows how to be vexed at evil and to rejoice, not immoderately, in lofty station. Such men as I are led by deliberate reason to live their lives correctly with the help of discretion. Now there are occasions when it is pleasant not to be too wise, and other occasions when it is good to have useful wits. I was reared in the abode of Chiron, a most righteous man, and so learned simplicity of character. And as for the sons of Atreus, if they show themselves good leaders, I will obey them; if not, I won't. Both here and at Troy I shall show my freedom of spirit, while so far as in me lies I do deeds of knightly daring. And as for thee, who hast been shamefully entreated by thy dearest, in so far as a young man may, so far will I enfold thee in my pity, and never shall thy daughter be slain by her father, when she hath been called mine; for I will not give my person to thy husband to weave his plots withal. For it is my name, even if it did not draw the sword, that will slaughter this thy child. The cause, to be sure, is thy husband; but myself will be no longer guiltless, if through me and marriage with me she must perish—she the damsel that hath suffered shamefully and intolerably, and hath in wondrous unworthy wise been dishonoured. I am the basest Greek alive; I, even I, am naught, and Menelaus is a true man; I am not the son of Peleus but of a fiend; if my name in thy husband's cause shall slaughter her! By Nereus I swear, Nereus reared amid the billows of the sea, the sire of Thetis my mother, that King Agamemnon shall not touch thy daughter, not even with his finger, not even touch her garment. Or Sipylus, on the frontiers of Heathenesse, the place from which these generals trace their descent, shall be a city, while Phthia, my own home, shall be forgotten on the earth. Calchas, the soothsayer, shall rue his sacrificial barley-meal and his holy water. Nay, what soothsayer is a man? Few truths he speaks, and many lies—and all by chance; then, when chance fails him, he is lost. Not because I wish for this marriage do I speak thus; thousands of girls pursue me for my hand. No; King Agamemnon has insulted me. He ought to have asked my permission that my name should be used to ensnare his child; it was the thought that I should be the bridegroom that tempted Clytæmnestra most. I would have granted this use of my name to the Greeks, if here lay the hitch in their voyage to Troy; I would not have refused to aid the common weal of my companions in arms. But now I am a cipher in the eyes of our generals—to treat me honourably or no is a light matter. Soon shall this sword make question, this sword which even before I come to Troy I will stain with slaughterous drops of gore, whether any man shall tear thy daughter from me. Keep quiet. I have appeared to thee a mighty god. I am not one. But I will be one.

"Was there ever such a fool?" you say. What a gloriously inept oration! Rodomontade and conceit, not even selfishness—it is nothing more. One is not surprised to hear that when Achilles appeals to the Greeks (probably in a similar harangue) they throw stones at him, and he comes rushing back to Clytæmnestra to report progress, or rather the lack of it. He again talks of fighting, but at this point Iphigenia, whose delicate nerves must have been hideously tried by all this beating of tom-toms, interferes and proclaims her readiness to die for the hopes of Greece. Achilles, after an awkward attempt at expressing his admiration, declares that he will none the less fight to save her. At the end of the play we learn that so far from doing this the loquacious champion has actually taken part in the ceremony of sacrifice: " the son of Peleus, with the basket and the holy water, ran round the altar of the goddess."

Both Achilles and Sergius Saranoff are made ridiculous, not necessarily by any fault of character, but by their attempt at critical moments, not to say what they feel, but to say what they think they ought to feel. Each has an impossible pose to keep up. Sergius, a thoroughly commonplace vulgar person, thinks he must talk like the mediæval knight and lover, merely because he is a military officer and has recently been in danger of his life. Achilles is a superficial spoiled young fellow, who has been taught that his mother is a goddess and who tries to live up to this impossible standard. He is too good a soldier not to know that any five (at most) of the Greeks are a match for him; but he has to make himself think that he can rout the whole host single-handed. Both these sawdust heroes deceive the audience for a long time, simply because of tradition. All the greater is the shock when the hero is found out; and it is not only the hero, but the cult of such people, which quivers under the blow. And that is precisely the aim both of Euripides and of Mr. Shaw.

Let me point to another parallel. These dramatists both handle the subject of revenge—the alleged unwritten law that those who are wronged but are prevented by the accident of law from seeking redress at the hands of the State, may, with perfect right, redress themselves. *Captain Brassbound's Conversion* is Shaw's study of this theory. Brassbound's mother has been neglected and cheated by her brother-in-law, an English judge. But nothing has been done against which the law can be reasonably invoked. The judge is respected as a model of respectability and uprightness; his nephew can do nothing save by stratagem and the help of luck. But luck does favour him. It so happens that Brassbound has the opportunity of taking Sir Howard into the

North African desert and there handing him over as a slave to an Arab chief. He proclaims his intention of doing so, hurling bitter reproaches and taunts at the judge, who thinks he has a right to rob his relatives and then to put on a robe of ermine and sentence his fellow-creatures to vindictive penalties under the name of legal punishment.

But Sir Howard's sister-in-law, Lady Cecily, is with the party. She talks to Brassbound as only a woman can who is a miracle of common sense and tact. Brassbound is made to see that his mission of vengeance is prompted far less by love for his mother than by hatred for his uncle, and that even if it were not, as his mother is dead, he can do nothing to help her now; moreover, that his whole life has been uselessly hardened and withered by brooding over his wrongs. But his quiver contains one more shaft: " It will teach other scoundrels to respect widows and orphans. Do you forget that there is such a thing as justice ? " To which Lady Cecily replies : " Oh, if you are going to dress yourself up in ermine and call yourself Justice, I give you up. You are just your uncle over again ; only he gets £5000 a year for it, and you do it for nothing." The whole drama leads to this conclusion, that revenge is a waste of energy and time, and worse. Bloodshed and oppression may be more intelligible if performed by way of reprisal; they are none the less offences against the true economy of society.

Such seems to be the moral of Euripides' *Electra* also, which deals with the most famous vendetta in Greek story. Agamemnon, after sacking Troy, returned to his home at Mycenæ in triumph, only to be murdered by his wife, Clytæmnestra, and her lover, Ægisthus. At the time of his death the King had two children—a daughter, Electra, and a son, Orestes, who was still a child. Electra, fearing for the heir to the throne, at once sent her brother across the border, herself remaining at home. Clytæmnestra and Ægisthus became joint rulers of the country. At length, when Orestes had grown to manhood, he was ordered by the Delphic oracle to go home and slay his mother and Ægisthus in requital for his father's murder. This he did, but avenging fiends, the Furies, pursued him for his matricide, until he was freed from them by Apollo.

Such is the story in outline—a magnificent subject for a playwright. But clearly the dramatist's point of view will make a world of difference. A poet penetrated by belief in the orthodox Olympian religion will lay tremendous stress on the fact that Orestes was impelled to his frightful deed by the direct and inevitable decree of Heaven; he will not admit the kinship between the victim and the slayer to be anything more than an important detail. This is the method which Æschylus has followed. Euripides' outlook is very different, even the opposite. In effect he says: "The kinship between the avenger and his victim is—must be—the cardinal point. If the oracle commanded Orestes to do this thing, so much the worse for the oracle." And so he insists on studying the grim old tale from the human standpoint, depicting, as does Shaw, the effects of a vendetta cherished for many years. Orestes, having lived abroad, has something (but not very much) of the many-sidedness which marks a well-developed man. But Electra all these years has lived on the thought of her murdered father and on the passionate thirst for more blood, even that of her mother. If Agamemnon has been murdered, that is no reason, the poet thinks, why his daughter should commit a slow moral suicide. She and her brother ruin their lives, as well as destroy their mother and Ægisthus, by their servility to a barren creed.

There is more than this. Both Shaw and Euripides have felt that, even granting the justice and wisdom of revenge, its pursuers can hold to their purpose only by keeping their eyes closed to some of the facts. It may be exaggeration to exclaim *tout comprendre c'est tout pardonner*, but every villain has some redeeming feature; nay, many "villains" are not villains at all. Quite legitimately, both writers have made their black sheep as white as possible. For Sir Howard Hallam there are real excuses enough to show us that he is at least as good as the average man. Brassbound himself at length declares : " My uncle is no worse a man than myself—better, most likely, for he has a better head and a higher place. Well, I took him for a villain out of a story-book."

What of Euripides ? He remembers that the murder of Agamemnon happened many years before. Why should not the murderers have become better instead of worse ?

A COMPARISON

And is not an act of revenge, like that of Orestes, carried out (as it had to be) by craft, necessarily repulsive? So it comes about that our sympathies are with Ægisthus and Clytæmnestra, not with their foes. Ægisthus is accosted by Orestes while on his farm celebrating a rustic sacrifice. He genially invites the strangers to join in the festival, and is struck dead from behind while engaged in an act of religion. Clytæmnestra is lured to her daughter's house by the most dastardly excuse which can be imagined. A message is sent to her that Electra has given birth to a child. It is Electra's own invention, which she thus expounds:

Announce that I have been delivered of a male child, ten days ago, and that the time of my purification is thus at hand. She will come when she hears that I have been through the pains of childbirth; aye, and she will weep over the low estate of my babe. Then when once she has come, of course, it is her death.

Could any speech, any situation, show more vividly the master-hand? In a few chill words it portrays the hideous poisoning of all natural love, sympathy, decency, which we noted a moment ago; it reminds us further that it is precisely because Electra has *not* had children that she can thus, in the course of years, be narrowed and blighted into a fiend; and it makes sure, not only that Clytæmnestra will come, but that she will come with just those emotions stirring her which make a woman most sincere and loving—at the moment when she is to be put to death, and that too by the help of one who should have been reminded, if not by her heart, yet by her own lie, how near and precious the victim should seem to her own children. The act of blood is performed, and the two awake to a tardy repentance, even then not reflecting that perhaps years ago their mother had her tardy repentance too.

One might offer many other such examples from Euripides of traditional heroes on whom the light of common day is poured with woeful results for the tinsel and sham jewellery—Jason, for instance; Jason whom so many generations have admired as the embodiment of chivalry, journeying to a far country in quest of the Fleece, that very symbol of romance, and from the edge of the world bringing with him Medea,

A COMPARISON

who left all for love. So have we all regarded Jason. But Euripides, whose interest in and sympathy for women surpassed that of any feminist of antiquity, prefers to ask himself what happened next. What of Jason as a married man, settled down to "getting on," with no definite profession and few assets beside the Golden Fleece? Could his wife prove a social success? Would she aid her husband's ambition by showing herself a tactful hostess and a *grande dame* in general? "Absurd," you say, "positively vulgar." Perhaps. And there is very real tragedy hovering round a haughty, noble, simple nature forced to live in an alien atmosphere. If Euripides chooses to interest himself in life as it is, rather than in magnificent episodes of the world's youth, you may call him Philistine if you will, but you cannot argue with a point of view. His treatment of this situation in the *Medea* is, perhaps, his greatest and most poignantly real work. The barbarian princess appears in the quiet aristocratic little courts of Greece like a destroying flame. At Iolchos, the home of Jason, she murders the old King Pelias, his enemy, by her savage cunning—the famous trick of the rejuvenating cauldron. Her husband and she, with their children, are forced to go into exile and find a home at Corinth. There Jason, still with no resources but his ancestry and his sword, determines to mend his fortunes by— marriage! His view, apparently, is that Medea is not exactly his wife—he is, indeed, very hazy about this—and that she ought not to object if, by a brilliant marriage, he secures his own prospects (for he intends to ally himself to the royal family) and incidentally hers and those of their children. Anyhow, Medea is only " a native." Learning his purpose, she breaks forth into passionate reproach and recital of all that she has done for him. Without her magical aid he would never have won the Fleece, nay, he could not have escaped from Colchis with his life. By thus assisting him she has been forced to leave her home and country, to entrust all her future to him. Jason is but little ruffled by this terrible appeal. He feels that the benefits she has wrought are indeed great—" You have not done badly," he remarks—but that the return he has already made is a full quittance; as thus :—

First of all, you live in Greece, instead of a barbarous land. You now understand justice and obedience to law, in place of arbitrary violence. Then, all the Greeks know of your wisdom and you have become a celebrity, whereas, if you had still been living at the end of the world, you would never have been heard of.

So might an impresario address a wonderful soprano whom he had " discovered " in Queensland or Dakota. We have travelled far indeed from the mediæval knight and his distressed damsel. The sequel, the frightful overthrow of all Jason's happiness and hopes, does not here concern us.

Let us now turn to our other topics. First of these must come social questions. On the Euripidean and Shavian treatment of this subject alone a volume could be written, but we shall here pass over it lightly. The two great social questions which attract Mr. Shaw beyond any other are the relations of the sexes and economic inequality: he is a feminist and a socialist. Euripides also is deeply concerned about such problems, but far more in the position of women than in that of the poor, for the sufficient reason that economic inequality seemed to him, and indeed was, less dangerous than the legal and social inequality of the sexes.

The reader does not need to be reminded of the industry and the wit which Mr. Shaw has expended upon the problems of poverty. Two whole plays are devoted to them—*Major Barbara* and *Widowers' Houses*. *John Bull's Other Island* and *Mrs. Warren's Profession* deal with the same theme, though there it is interwoven with other matters, in the first with imperial politics and in the second with the sex-question. Whatever one thinks of Mr. Shaw's conclusions, no one save a partisan journalist can deny the sincerity and the public spirit of his method and aims. That which in Euripides corresponds to this feature of Shaw's work is his indignation, not so much against financial inequality as against political inequality and bureaucracy. He loves to inveigh against officials, whether they are rulers and generals, or whether they are mere Bumbles, and he is never weary of praising the middle class. The poet seems to have been a very moderate democrat. He distrusts the rich and nobly-born, but he also fears the masses. Probably he would have liked to see a return to the

Solonian regime, to give *prima facie* political equality to all citizens, with the important reservation that the archonship and the board of generals should be filled from certain classes only. Against the oligarchy of the rich and the anarchy of the mob the middle class, according to him, formed an effective, and the only, safeguard.

More startling than this, to an Athenian at any rate, was his championship of slaves. The statement of Aristotle, a man almost as broad-minded as profound, that a slave is a living tool, expresses the popular opinion and the legal view. Euripides is apparently the only man of his day who showed any sort of real sympathy for slaves; his nameless messengers, attendants, old men, and the like, form a noble company of obscure and faithful ones.

But by far the strongest claim of Euripides to renown as a social theorist is his study of women—their character, their actual position in society, and their possibilities. It is a feature in the work of this dramatist which, before any other attribute, has arrested attention in his own day and in every other age in which he has been intelligently studied; it accounts, probably, for several anecdotes about his life. There is hardly a single extant tragedy of his which does not contain some wonderfully penetrating and illuminating study of female character. But far more than this: several of his finest works are devoted primarily, almost exclusively, to this theme—the *Medea*, the *Hippolytus*, the *Alcestis*, and the *Andromache*. In all these instances Euripides' opinions and emotions are plain and expressed with admirable incisiveness; and in all he is observing, not the heroine of legend, but the contemporary Athenian woman. In all, too, he is striving to create a more healthy public opinion. It has been said that " of all ancient moralists, he is alone, or alone with Plato, in showing an *adequate* notion of that radical disease, an imperfect ideal of woman, of which, more than of anything else, ancient civilization perished." Against this disease no man except Plato struggled so bravely as Euripides, and not even Plato with equal discernment.

It is not so much that he admires women, still less that he regards them as superior to men; his subtle and true delineations bring out as many faults as virtues. He is impressed by two things: first, the sorrows of women, whether they arise from the indifference of individuals and of the State, or whether they are the special pains and hardships which no reform can lift from their shoulders; second, the danger to the community which lies in allowing a great mass of persons to pass their lives and spend their energies within its borders without attempting to understand them, without forming some sort of working hypothesis, good or bad, about their function as a part of the community—without, in short, *digesting* them. He thinks of women as a man of human sympathies, and as a citizen of political foresight.

In describing the sorrows of women, then, Euripides shows a knowledge of the female heart which excites the liveliest interest and wonder. We are told that he was twice married, and unhappily. Unhappy his married life may have been according to the gossips, but there is good evidence that the poet talked to his wife, and more, that he let her talk to him; still more, that while she talked he listened. No man unaided could have written that marvellous first speech of Medea, a foreigner at Corinth, seeing herself and her young children on the point of being deserted by Jason. She is addressing the company of Corinthian ladies who have come to condole with her.

Now, as for me, this unlooked-for happening hath broken my heart. Friends, I am lost. The joy of life hath left me, and I fain would die. For, as ye know well, he, my husband, in whom were all my hopes, hath shown himself an utter villain. Of all creatures that have life and reason we women are the most unhappy. For, first, by payment of much wealth we must needs purchase a husband, a master of our persons. . . . And herein lies a fearful peril: will he be base or good ? For the wife is disgraced by divorce, yet to refuse marriage is impossible. Then, when a woman has come to live with a strange character and strange ways of life, she must needs have second-sight (for her past experience tells her nothing) if she is to know how to deal with her husband. If, then, we solve this riddle, and the spouse who dwells with us proves not a brutal yoke-fellow, our life is to be envied; otherwise, death were best. When a man is wearied of his home, he walks abroad and relieves his spirit of its distaste in the society of some friend or companion; but we are forced to look to one person only. And they say of us that we pass within the house a life unthreatened by any peril, whereas they engage in the toil of war. Fools! I had rather fight three pitched battles than face the pains of childbirth once. But no more. What is true of me cannot be said of thee. Thou hast this city and thy father's house, a happy life, and the company of friends; while I, deserted and homeless, am outraged by my husband, I that have been reft from a foreign land and have no mother, no brother, no kinsman, to whom, as to a haven, I may flee from this calamity. This, then, will I ask of thee, this only. If I discover some means, some plot, whereby to win revenge for these my wrongs from my husband, from him that gave his daughter, and from herself, be silent. In all things else a woman is full of dread and dares not look upon battles and the sword; but if she is wronged in her affections, there is no other soul so bloodthirsty.

Nothing need, or can by me, be added to the earlier part of this. It is only one example among many that could be cited of the poet's subtle sympathy and understanding of women—an understanding, no doubt, helped by his love for children; the yearning of a parent over his child has never been expressed more poignantly than by a few verses in this very play of *Medea*. But observe particularly the last few words in which Medea hints to the Corinthian ladies that she has a plan of vengeance. It is in this way that the great speech which I have tried to render brings us to the second part of this subject, Euripides' feeling that the contemporary attitude towards women was a menace to society. He understood the frightful explosive force of a nature adult in its passions, its will, its audacity, but in intellectual weakness and unbalanced impulsiveness a child. At all costs, he felt, we must recast our social system; we must open to women activities which can give their natures space to develop healthily. I suspect that he would have assented to the epigram which declares that " the last thing man will civilize is woman "; but the longer Athens put off the attempt the greater was the danger. This belief, that the harem-system which prevailed at Athens was a real peril, appears repeatedly. In the *Andromache* he is principally concerned to show us the evil which may be wrought by an impulsive untrained woman, denied all interest in outside things but allowed despotic power in her own house. The curse of the Athenian system was, according to him, that it stunted all a woman's good qualities, while it left her free to indulge her cruel or thoughtless whims. To quote the *Medea* once more, the female sex is called " helpless for good, but of all mischief plotters most cunning." As in that play he has painted a woman of pride and courage goaded by her wrongs into crime, so in the *Andromache* he presents us with a weaker, more febrile, girl led by her own unguided impulses—still into crime.

Two remarks should here be offered. The first is that Euripides' lesson applies, at the utmost, only partly to us. On any view, the condition of women is not now so spiritually and intellectually debased as it was in Athens during the fifth century B.C. The second remark is still more germane to our subject. Allowing for differences in circumstances, it can be said that Mr. Shaw takes up much the same position as Euripides. Those who have read that powerful and terrible drama, *Mrs. Warren's Profession*, will remember that Mrs. Warren devotes herself to the basest and most anti-social of all trades just because she is forced into it by the social and economic conditions which make everything else but starvation impossible. *Man and Superman*, magnificent as it is, need not detain us now. No comparison with the work of Euripides is here possible, as the play is based on a conception of woman which was a sheer impossibility to any Greek of classical days.

It is time that we turned to a very obvious feature of both these writers—a feature observed by the most casual reader, and sometimes held to be Mr. Shaw's single literary virtue. I mean the directness, wit, and athletic brilliance of their style. From Euripides one may select a fine piece of invective uttered by the captive Andromache, the widow of Hector, when she has been shamefully lured to her death by the King of Sparta:—

> Ye hated wretches, spurned of all mankind,
> Tenants of Sparta, souls of crawling craft,
> Plotters of villainy and lords of lies,
> Whose souls are rotten, yea, a labyrinth
> Of cheating, this your glory 'mid the Greeks
> On sin is founded and by sin has thriven!
> What foulness know ye not? Love ye not blood
> And shameful gains? Are ye not ever found
> With lips confirming what your hearts deny?
> Curses upon you! But, for me, my death
> Hath lost its sting—thou'rt cheated. *Then* I died
> When hapless Troy was taken, and my lord
> Fell like a chieftain, he whose spear full oft
> Chased thee from land to quake upon thy ship.
> Now, lo! thou'rt come in panoply of war
> To fright a woman, and to slay me. Aye,
> Slay on! These lips shall never beg my life
> From child of thine or fawn on such as thou!
> Mighty art thou in Sparta? So was I
> Erstwhile at Troy. And if I fall to-day,
> Forbear thy vaunts. Soon may'st thou fall as low.

A COMPARISON

Or take this passage from the *Iphigenia at Aulis*, in which the young princess makes her magnificent avowal that she is ready to die that she may give the Greek fleet a fair wind for Troy :—

Hellas, mightiest of nations, now on me bends all her gaze;
I can ope the broad Ægean, I can Ilion's towers raze!
I can drown in blood of Trojans Helen's flight and Paris' crime;
I can school each lewd barbarian, through the years of after-time,
Ne'er again to steer his pinnace to the happy shores of Greece.
Dying, I shall save a nation, and my fame shall aye increase,
Raising me in death to greatness, Hellas' saviour, blest indeed.
Nay, 'twere ill my life to cherish, shunning thus for her to bleed.
I was born the child of Hellas, not, O mother, only thine.
See, ten thousand armèd heroes! See their linkèd bucklers' line!
See ten thousand straining oarsmen, every heart with courage high,
Ready in their country's quarrel to avenge her wrongs or die!
Shall the life of one weak woman baffle all this fair emprise?
Nay, 'twere sin! What guiltless answer to our falt'ring lips could rise?
Think once more! Achilles yonder, would'st thou see him strive—and fall—
Battling with the host of Argos single-handed at my call?
Twere a gain one man should live, were e'en ten thousand maids the price.
Yea, and Artemis demands my body to her sacrifice.
When the hand divine hath beckoned, shall a mortal shun her fate?

Never! To the hopes of Hellas I my being consecrate.
Slay me! Vanquish Troy! I die not childless, since through ages down
Lives, in place of home and children, this my never-dimmed renown!

From Mr. Shaw's work let us select this fine piece of declamation from *Cæsar and Cleopatra*. Julius Cæsar, walking alone by night across the Egyptian desert, comes upon the Sphinx:—

Hail, Sphinx: salutation from Julius Cæsar! I have wandered in many lands, seeking the lost regions from which my birth into this world exiled me, and the company of creatures such as I myself. I have found flocks and pastures, men and cities, but no other Cæsar, no air native to me, no man kindred to me, none who can do my day's deed, and think my night's thought. In the little world yonder, Sphinx, my place is as high as yours in this great desert; only I wander, and you sit still; I conquer, and you endure; I work and wonder, you watch and wait; I look up and am dazzled, look down and am darkened, look round and am puzzled, whilst your eyes never turn from looking out—out of the world—to the lost region—the home from which we have strayed. Sphinx, you and I, strangers to the race of men, are no strangers to one another: have I not been conscious of you and of this place since I was born? Rome is a mad-

A COMPARISON

man's dream: this is my reality. These starry lamps of yours I have seen from afar in Gaul, in Britain, in Spain, in Thessaly, signalling great secrets to some eternal sentinel below, whose post I never could find. And here at last is their sentinel—an image of the constant and immortal part of my life, silent, full of thought, alone in the silver desert.

Lastly, here is a trenchant passage from *Major Barbara*. The self-made millionaire is discussing with his aristocratic son the profession which the latter should choose. After several of his suggestions have been declined, the father goes to the point :—

UNDERSHAFT : Well, come ! Is there *anything* you know or care for ?
STEPHEN : I know the difference between right and wrong.
UNDERSHAFT : You don't say so ! What ! No capacity for business, no knowledge of law, no sympathy with art, no pretension to philosophy ; only a simple knowledge of the secret that has puzzled all the philosophers, baffled all the lawyers, muddled all the men of business, and ruined most of the artists : the secret of right and wrong. Why, man, you're a genius, a master of masters, a god ! At twenty-four, too !
STEPHEN : You are pleased to be facetious. I pretend to nothing more than any honour-

able English gentleman claims as his birthright.

UNDERSHAFT: Oh, that's everybody's birthright. Look at poor little Jenny Hill, the Salvation lassie! She would think you were laughing at her if you asked her to stand up in the street and teach grammar or geography or mathematics or even drawing-room dancing; but it never occurs to her to doubt that she can teach morals and religion. You are all alike, you respectable people. You can't tell me the bursting strain of a ten-inch gun, which is a very simple matter; but you all think you can tell me the bursting strain of a man under temptation. You daren't handle high explosives; but you're all ready to handle honesty and truth and justice and the whole duty of man, and kill one another at that game. What a country! What a world!

Finally, there is a likeness between these two men in the treatment they have received from their contemporaries. That both have attracted vast attention is a point which needs no proof; but combined with this we notice a strong reaction. Euripides produced plays at Athens for about fifty years; only five times was he awarded the first prize in the dramatic contest, and one of these victories was obtained after his death. The official leaders of public opinion

A COMPARISON

scouted him; men in their position could not support a writer who habitually ridiculed the claims of the Delphic oracle, who showed scant respect even for Athena, the guardian-goddess of the State, who hated officialism, who discussed at large the rights and the feelings of mere slaves, who appeared to think that women had souls, perhaps even a social value, who was for ever examining and condemning the most revered traditions, who was, in short, "queer." We have learned from a recently-discovered manuscript that he was indicted by the statesman Cleon for impiety. The chief voice of this hostility was the comic dramatist Aristophanes, as great a genius as Euripides himself, whose magnificent comedy of *The Frogs* is in the main an elaborate attack upon Euripides' teaching, and who is never weary of directing laughable and trenchant gibes against the great apostle of rationalism.

Much the same is the position of Mr. Shaw. No statesman brings him to trial for impiety, perhaps because we do not agree as to what piety is; but the rôle of Aristophanes is filled with painstaking emulation by the Press. It must be allowed that the onslaughts of our journalists are not so brilliant or so searching as those of the Athenian dramatist, but they do their best. Failing the genius of Aristophanes, they fall back on his unfairness and his sneers. To judge from *The Frogs* one would suppose Euripides, not a great but misguided and misguiding poet; rather a mere scribbling, pernicious fool. A weekly review of the highest standing published an article on one of Mr. Shaw's volumes in which the word "jester" was employed a dozen times. It is a significant word. The English publicist knows well that the shortest way to rob a man of influence is to call him amusing, the rooted belief of the British public being that if a man is funny he cannot be in earnest. Accordingly Mr. Shaw is dubbed "the licensed jester"—that is to say: "This is a funny man; therefore you may read and enjoy him without feeling bound to pay any respect to what he says." And the newspapers have one vast advantage over Aristophanes. Few men in Athens took him seriously, while to-day most people are positively hypnotized by whatever they see in print if only it is repeated often enough. And it is repeated, very often. The deliberate and unending misrepresentation of

Mr. Shaw by hosts of journalists who know better is a public scandal.

Still, there is another side to the picture. That Euripides should be hated by Cleon, and Shaw despised by Broadbent, is natural enough. They have both found a recompense in the delighted respect of their younger contemporaries. What especially annoyed Aristophanes was the unbounded influence which Euripides wielded over educated young men. The future was with him, and during the centuries which have passed since his death few Greek writers have enjoyed so continuous and discriminating a popularity. When the contest in the world of the dead, the contest between Æschylus and Euripides portrayed in *The Frogs*, is about to begin, Æschylus complains that he is at a disadvantage because he has left his works on earth alive, while his rival's plays have died with him. Never was a prophecy more utterly refuted by time. It is not unreasonable to prophesy similar permanence for the dramas of Mr. Shaw. No work will die which is so instinct with wit, with breadth of mind and lively interest, with such a passionate zeal for the common health. Already, as did his

Athenian counterpart, he is coming into his kingdom; no name stands higher with educated people of the new generation than his. And this assures his popularity and his influence for future time; as years go by he will be more respectfully studied and more highly valued. He can repeat, as Euripides might have done, the words uttered by one of Schiller's characters: "The century is not ripe for my ideal. I live a citizen of a future commonwealth."

THE PRESENT RENAISSANCE OF ENGLISH DRAMA

BETWEEN the year 1779, in which Sheridan's *Critic* was produced, and the year 1889, when *A Doll's House* was first performed in England, lies the Dark Age of our dramatic literature. During those hundred and ten years the theatres themselves had flourished, and first-rate actors had not been rare; but the art of dramatic composition lay in torpor. While the novel attained glory in the hands of Scott, Thackeray, and Dickens, the most noted writers for the stage were Joanna Baillie, Thomas Robertson, Dion Boucicault, and Westland Marston. Of all the theatrical matter produced in that period by writers no longer living, there are perhaps only two works which the playgoing public has not completely forgotten—Robertson's *Caste* and *David Garrick*. The censorship established by Walpole in 1737 had warned men of genius off the stage. Fielding is a celebrated instance; what the novel gained, playwriting lost. But where original genius was forbidden to tread, Robertson and his congeners rushed in. The result was horrible. One might harrow up the reader's soul with extracts from the works which for four generations degraded the theatre of Vanbrugh and Sheridan into the abyss where the disciples of Ibsen found it.

But he shall be spared such an anthology. Only let him imagine the most difficult form of literary art, where architectonic power is essential, where so much depends upon the collision of genuine personalities, upon sound ethics and skill in language. Imagine the law thus laid down for the writer who is to practise such an art. "You shall not discuss religion, though you may occasionally employ its more orthodox forms as part of your upholstery. Politics are to be eschewed, unless you wish to remind your hearers of the glory of Britain—we shall not object to a few honest tars or even to a comic soldier, provided he is of non-commissioned rank. Satire of course is permitted, except that you must satirize only people who have been satirized already—a lawyer, provided he is only an attorney; a politician, so long as he is not a Minister; a farmer, but mind you demonstrate the goodness of his heart. What? You complain that we are shackling your inventive genius? Nothing of the kind! You can portray society. Show us the great heart of the English People—of course without hurting anyone's feelings, for you will remember that you are a gentleman. Literature should uplift. Therefore you will teach us that love is always unselfish, that men in high positions have characters to correspond, that dramatic heroes are unswervingly muscular, tall, brave, and generous. Marriages are always happy; children are always obedient, except in farces, and then, fortunately, they have idiotic fathers, whom you can't expect them to take seriously; there are only two sorts of women—(*a*) ladies, who invariably behave *as* ladies; and (*b*) females, who can be relied upon for a little comic relief."

Finally, conceive this difficult art practised, under such poisonous restrictions, by men of third-rate or fourth-rate talent. One pretentious writer after another came forward, not with a " slice of life," as the saying now is, not even with a self-consistent romantic fantasy, but with an exercise in the theatrical manner. That is the real vice of the stage—to copy the latest "successful" play instead of looking at men and women. This is what is meant by staginess —not merely the striking of attitudes: Shakespeare is full of them; not simply long speeches: Mr. Shaw revels in them, and Mr. Barker's Trebell is a leading article on two legs. No; it is the unmistakable imitation of an imitation. Those who objected to stage plays as immoral would have stood on much firmer ground had they accused them of a paralysing dullness.

Precisely one hundred years after Sheridan's success with *The Critic*, Copenhagen witnessed the production of *A Doll's House*. Ten years later, after triumphs in Scandinavia and Germany, the play was given in London by Mr. Charles Charrington and Miss Janet Achurch. "It was this production that really made Ibsen known to the English-speaking peoples," says Mr. William Archer. By this play and by his other "realist" works, such as *An Enemy of the People*, *Rosmersholm*, *The Wild Duck*, Ibsen, single-handed, saved English drama at the moment. I say "at the moment," for even had there been no Ibsen, one cannot believe that the

English nation would have battened till doomsday upon works like *Caste* or *The Hobbyhorse*. But to Ibsen, alone of individual men, belongs the credit of the fact that we now possess real dramatists. What are his special virtues, the lineaments of his genius ?

As a dramatic poet, Ibsen stands beyond question in the front rank. Setting himself to produce a certain form of art, he has reached an achievement as near perfection as that of Sophocles or Shakespeare ; *Hedda Gabler*, in its *genre*, is as great as *Œdipus Rex* or *Macbeth* in theirs. We are, of course, to note that the *genre* is different. Neglect of this simple fact vitiated all the judgments which English critics offered upon the new writer in the last years of the nineteenth century. What they meant was that Ibsen is not like Robertson, to say nothing of Shakespeare. In the same way French critics who worshipped Aristotle's canons of tragic art declared that Shakespeare was a drunken savage. One remembers the even more idiomatic criticism in *Punch* : " There's a stranger ! 'Eave 'arf a brick at 'im ! " Every insulting adjective that the printer could be induced to put into type was hurled at the stranger when *Ghosts* was performed in 1891. People were simply blaming him for not possessing qualities which would have prevented them from ever hearing about him, for not following a fashion which it was his chief aim to eradicate. The *genre* of *Hedda Gabler* is different from that of any other school. Whether it is as sublime and edifying a type as that of the Elizabethan and of the Greek tragedians is quite a different matter. It is, in any case, a magnificent creation, capable of values which can be attained in no other way. In brief, the aim of Sophocles was to make man accommodate his intellect to his spiritual environment; the aim of Shakespeare to entertain by chastening the emotions; the aim of Ibsen to instruct by a new appeal to ethical facts.

This brings us to the first salient characteristic of the Norwegian—his courage. He never runs away from facts in life, nor from the situations which he himself portrays. The customary procedure being to get over a difficulty by pretending that it does not exist, Ibsen not only proves that it does exist, but also—a vital point—that it is only by ignoring it that we give it full power over us. Nor does he shrink from the consequences of his own imagination. There is nothing which the third-rate dramatist loves better than the attempt to make the best, so to speak, of both worlds—to win approbation from the stalls by a daring scene, and then run away from it, to snatch the cheers of the gallery. So, in *The Notorious Mrs. Ebbsmith,* Sir Arthur Pinero depicts a spirited, hard-driven woman who, at a crisis, is offered a Bible. She flings it into the fire. " Here ! " says the culture-hunter, " is courage of one's convictions. Here is an advanced playwright ! And how advanced of me to be here ! Pinero and I are making history." But Mrs. Ebbsmith utters a scream. It cannot be ! She rushes to the stove and drags forth the volume, brandishing it aloft amid the ecstasies of the gods. Here is "something for everyone," in truth ! Ibsen, of course, like every other dramatist worth his salt, never dreams of thus running with the hare and hunting with the hounds. Compromise may be the life of politics, but it is the death of art. Ibsen's own uncompromising honesty has led to queer results, not the least odd being the history of *A Doll's House.* In that celebrated conversation between Nora and Torvald Helmer with which the play ends, it is of course essential that the wife should stick to her guns, quietly but with complete assurance. When the play reached Germany, theatrical managers actually provided it with a "happy ending," in which Nora did not leave her husband after all, and the famous slam of the door, the neatest and most legitimate *coup de théâtre* in the history of the stage, was left out! At that time his works had no protection in Germany, and the master himself was driven to devise, for the moment, another finale in which Nora, for her children's sake, remained at home. He explained that he "preferred to commit the outrage himself." His revenge was signal and almost laughably appropriate. The very next work he wrote was *Ghosts*, in which the wife did *not* leave her husband. The results of that wifely compliance were so horrible that for many years *Ghosts* lay under the veto of the English censor.

I allude merely in passing to the splendid reality of his character-drawing and the pungency of his situations, so terrifying in their earnestness and sincerity, so purifying and regenerating in proportion to their ruthlessness. Another side of his genius is the architectonic skill by which he rivals the Athenian masters. He knows hardly anything of underplots; there is not a scene or a character, hardly a word, which is not a stone in a simple edifice—always necessary, always adequate for the advancement of the one purpose. As to his subject-matter, he is (so far as England at any rate is concerned) the father of the so-called " drama of ideas," but he himself belongs to that school only in the most general sense. Ibsen has no social theory or political propaganda or religious or ethical dogma, of any very specialized sort, to advance. No specific abuses or temporary " causes " claim him as their opponent or champion. He is too fundamental for that; what he writes is written *sub specie æternitatis*. He wishes us to revise our attitude towards life, to change our notion of values. By him we are taught, as by all great teachers, not so much what to think as how to think, not action but the reasoned basis of action. An ingenuous tyro, who should study these dramas in order to cleanse his way, would be perplexed to find that in *An Enemy of the People* truth-speaking at all costs is Stockmann's duty, whereas in *The Wild Duck* it wrecks a home and kills an innocent, affectionate child; that in *Hedda Gabler* a wife shoots herself in order (as it appears) to avoid the importunities of a lover, while in *Ghosts* a woman who has been saved from infidelity traces all the misfortunes of her family to her own lack of initiative. But the secret is that, for Ibsen and his followers, the spring of action is not conventional morals, but a far-seeing economy of happiness; it has been admirably expressed by Mr. Shaw: "The real slavery of to-day is slavery to ideals of goodness." Dogmatic morality is an idol, prompting mere waste of character and energy. The only criterion of goodness in an act is its effect on happiness. If morality demands that one should sacrifice one's happiness and usefulness, so much the worse for morality. Many of the furious cavalry-charges, which have flung themselves upon his lines, are in one sense justified. Those who say he is immoral are right, but it does not follow that they are right in objecting to his immorality. Morals are the codified expression of the current behaviour of the day. A man who breaks the code may be wicked; he may equally well be the apostle of a new morality, whose first duty is to challenge the old. The whole mistake of the early attacks upon Ibsen was that people took him for a law-breaker of the first type, whereas he belongs to the second. Such teaching as his must of course be dangerous, like all exploring expeditions; a path is to be made through a jungle infested by savage beasts. And there will be camp-followers to disgrace the march, because they have joined, not for exploration, but for plunder.

Such, in brief, are the doctrine and methods of Ibsen. What are their effects in England? The native playwrights of our time form a highly variegated band, but it may be divided with fair accuracy into four divisions. One may here be dismissed summarily though respectfully—the school represented by the late Stephen Phillips and by Mr. Gordon Bottomley. Though much of their work is magnificent, a discussion of "the present renaissance" must pass them by, since they have devoted themselves to the "poetical" drama and are manifestly in the technical tradition of Browning and Tennyson, with little or no specific relation to the spirit of our own time. The second category, by far the most popular and influential, practises an artificial and theatrical criticism of contemporary manners. Of this school the most notable members to-day are Sir Arthur Pinero and Mr. Henry Arthur Jones. The third category contains only Mr. John Masefield. To the fourth belong Mr. Granville Barker, Mr. Galsworthy, Mr. Shaw, and, of deceased writers, George Calderon and St. John Hankin. Let us discuss these last three divisions in turn.

The first finds its "Morning Star" in Oscar Wilde, who, if cleverness could suffice for drama, would have been the greatest master since Congreve of the Comedy of Manners. *The Importance of Being Earnest* is perhaps the best farce in existence, exemplifying to admiration Wilde's magnificence of epigram, elegance of language, deadness of soul. What could be better than the prospective mother-in-law's dismay at finding that the suitor is a foundling, a man whose career began by being discovered in a handbag? "You can hardly imagine that I and Lord Bracknell would dream of allowing our only daughter—a girl brought up with the utmost care—to marry into a cloakroom, and form an alliance with a parcel?" The same brilliance is lavishly spread over his serious plays. Perhaps the finest epigram in the world occurs in *Lady Windermere's Fan*: "What is a cynic?" —"A man who knows the price of everything and the value of nothing." But is this drama? It does not help the action, it throws little light on the character of the man who utters it; Lord Darlington is only a name, though one of the chief personages in the play. That particular scene is a celebrated blaze of epigrams. "Wicked women bother one, good women bore one. That is the only difference between them." "Scandal is gossip made tedious by morality." "In this world there are only two tragedies. One is not getting what one wants. The other is getting it." But an orgy of confectionery is not a solid meal, nor are these decadent blossoms capable of making a play. Wilde's characters are feeble utterly — either comic, pouring forth brassy wit in season and out of season; or serious, mere gramophones emitting platitudes on love, honour, or social service. The old theatrical situations which satisfied Robertson and Westland Marston, the strained improbable crises unreally handled, furbished up by a peerless gift of wit in order to impress the uncritical with a sense of ultra-modernity—such is his work. We see him now as essentially commonplace, a verdict which would have sent him into a swoon.

Wilde is the earliest and most brilliant member of what we may call the Neo-British School. Succeeding writers do, to be sure, exhibit special qualities, but the seal of Wilde is upon them all. They are, in short, the heirs of Robertson, who have latterly obtained a spurious appearance of freshness by a pretence of following Ibsen or by a half-hearted attempt to follow him. In the Robertsonian era the formula ran thus. Take a simple love-story—a girl with beauty and a heart of gold, a man in a cavalry uniform; this will charm the audience into accepting any improbability of detail. Next we insert dramatic effect. This is done by attaching to one of the lovers an incongruous parent. (In *Caste* there are two, the lady's drunken father and the hero's Plantagenet mother; hence the long-continued vogue of the whole.) The incongruous parent causes fun and trouble. As a foil or antidote to him, introduce a humble friend, who by dropping his (or her) aitches will evince the goodness of his (or her) heart. Punctuation consists in making your " immaculate swell " sit on his silk hat. An " effective curtain " to each act is secured by the mechanical intrusion of something to make the audience jump. Let the tipsy friend reel in and offer the Duchess his mug of beer. Or the postman (that most hard-worked of all theatrical characters) will ring the bell; and the curtain goes down to " We are ordered to India ! " or " Thank Heaven, my child is found ! "

Most members of the Neo-British School are aware that this kind of writing will not do without some kind of disguise or revision. For one thing, mere repetition has made it stale beyond endurance. For another, most of them have far too much intellect and sense of artistic decency to be content with the well-nigh incredible badness of the typical mid-nineteenth-century play. And, thirdly, there is Ibsen to count with; people may hate or despise or misunderstand Ibsen as much as they please, but after seeing a work of his they are no longer quite so satisfied with their own favourite play or type of play. Accordingly, the Neo-British

School is pseudo-Ibsenist or (if that sounds too offensive) quasi-Ibsenist; for one should distinguish between those who have merely picked up Ibsenian tricks and those who are really seeking to learn from him something new about life and art. Our one reason for placing these latter in our second category and not in our fourth is precisely this, that Ibsen's influence upon them has been too intermittent or slight for them to break with dramatic Victorianism.

Accordingly the method of this school is to write a play thoroughly conventional at heart, and to tag it out with details or flourishes which look like Ibsenism. The audience finds nothing to cause hostility or misgiving, and yet it has a delicious sense of being in the movement, of facing the music. Take the old Robertsonian formula, but instead of a hero in the Heavy Dragoons give us a hero in shirt-sleeves; instead of militiamen, talk of aviation; and don't make all your foreigners either fools or scoundrels. You will then win the respect due to antiquity together with the admiration deserved by originality. Thus Mr. Rudolf Besier's play, *Don*, made a notable stir. There is the framework of a gentle scholarly ecclesiastic and his wife, both devoted to their brilliant son; the "choleric" old general and his wife, with a sweet wise daughter. The brilliant son and the sweet wise daughter are, one learns with small astonishment, engaged to be married. But now let us show we have a sense of the *Zeitgeist*. Instead of a comic Irishman or the sale of military plans to a foreign foe, let us depict a domestic problem. The son therefore runs away with a married woman. Your pseudo-advanced writer invariably reveals his calibre by this assumption that the "problem-play" must treat of marital infidelity: there is only one sin—the Decalogue has become a monologue. But it must be owned that Mr. Besier has achieved novelty, since the brilliant son aforesaid has eloped for quite "innocent" reasons. The lady has a positive bogey-man for a husband, whose extraordinary bristliness is killing her. The hero, a most unworldly person, feels that she must be taken away for a little rest and petting; he brings her to his own home, and hands her over to his mother. The husband pursues, and there follows an elaborate contest between the gentle ecclesiastic (who positively reeks of Christchurch) and the fanatical Nonconformist ranter. Such is pseudo-Ibsenism, as shown by a favourable specimen, for Mr. Besier is almost the best writer of the whole school; his dialogue and situations, in *Don* at any rate, do not smell of the footlights.

A good deal of this praise must be given also to Mr. Alfred Sutro, who in an amiable, light-hearted, not too vigorous way has given us credible and sincerely - written scenes. But one cannot help feeling that his work is actually composed in a theatre; there is too much of Wilde's artificial gloss. It is somewhat quaint that Mr. Sutro's best piece should be actually named *The Man in the Stalls*. Mr. Somerset Maugham's work has on the whole about the same value as Mr. Sutro's, but he varies far more in excellence. At one time he was terribly unreal, the Robertson of an England which supposed that when good Britons died they went to Monte Carlo. At that period he was perhaps the most repellently stagey of the whole Neo-British School; it is almost incredible that *Jack Straw* was produced as recently as 1908; the play is obsolete beyond words, except that the foreign ambassador speaks excellent English — a daring stroke which reveals Mr. Maugham upon his watch-tower, reporting the time of day. Since then he has become equal to Mr. Sutro; *The Land of Promise*, despite the rather violent severance of its first act from the others, is good, forceful drama. Mr. Arnold Bennett, in *The Honeymoon, Milestones,* and *The Title,* has shown some charm, originality, and " sense of the theatre," but on the whole he has mildly and unexcitingly followed the Neo-British manner.

There remain three members of this category whose dramatic reputation with the majority of playgoers stands far higher. Sir J. M. Barrie has charmed us all so poignantly with his marvellous *Peter Pan*— which is by this time not so much a play as an institution, like *Alice in Wonderland*— that one finds difficulty in considering him as a dramatist. But most of his work consists of traditional ideas aerated by a novel *mise-en-scène* (as in *The Admirable Crichton*) —the ethical and emotional standards of a novelette draped in raiment of delightful hue and texture. Mr. Henry Arthur Jones has far more dramatic force and sincerity;

he is, indeed, rightly regarded as the finest playwright of this school. As Mr. Jones vigorously repudiates Ibsen, for instance in the preface to his *Divine Gift*, and as he undoubtedly possesses technical skill of a high order combined with a genuine interest in ethical truth, one hesitates to attribute his progress in stage-mastery and pungency to Ibsen's influence. But he is none the less Neo-British. His ideas are striking and presented by excellent situations; but the treatment of them, despite admirable *aperçus* by the way, peters out into conventional moralizing and futility. In *The Philistines, The Liars, Michael and his Lost Angel*, we feel that we are witnessing a play, not a picture of life.

Thus do we finally reach the portentous Sir Arthur Pinero. Of all contemporary English dramatists whom one can take seriously he is the most popular, the most prolific, and the most meretricious; one cannot imagine the action in his plays as happening in any but artificial light. His earliest published work, *The Magistrate* (revived as *The Boy*), is perhaps the best. Granted the old conventions of impossible misunderstandings, amazing and endless coincidences, this farce is distinctly good; "Gone—and without a cry—brave fellow!" is an inspiration. But when one considers that the plot hinges on the imposture of a mother who for her own sake knocks off several years from her son's age, with the result that a stripling of more or less marriageable age is presented as a boy young enough to be kissed and petted by various ladies, who one and all accept the fraud without murmur—when one considers this, one cannot award Sir Arthur any very impressive laurels. *The Magistrate* is, however, his cleverest play; of the others we cannot attempt to give a catalogue. But although Sir Arthur, in a letter prefaced to Mr. W. L. Courtney's *Idea of Tragedy*, mentions with very scant respect the greatest playwright since Shakespeare, his work is the most instructive example that could be chosen of Ibsen's influence on the Neo-British School. Noticing the vogue which the incomprehensible Norwegian was gaining, even in London, Sir Arthur Pinero seems to have exclaimed, "Britons never shall be slaves!" and produced *The Second Mrs. Tanqueray* and *The Notorious Mrs. Ebbsmith*. The latter person has been discussed earlier. As for her colleague, Mrs. Tanqueray, the author has sat down to devise a "strong scene" in the most advanced style—the conversation between the stepmother and the man who is her stepdaughter's accepted suitor, and whose mistress the stepmother herself has been. All the rest of the piece is scaffolding, and the climax itself, failing of real cogency and pathos, becomes merely sordid and vexatious. The truth is that Pinero is amazingly trivial. *Preserving Mr. Panmure* deals with a governess who is kissed against her will, and the whole action consists of complications caused by the fact that she will not reveal the identity of her admirer (her employer) while her employer's wife insists on trying to discover which of their guests is guilty. And to this theme the dramatist devotes, not one act, but four!

Mr. Masefield's position is utterly different. In downright genius he is one of the greatest Englishmen now engaged upon literature. In *Pompey the Great* we have simply a good theatrical history-play. But *The Tragedy of Nan* is a drama of extraordinary merit. It is so sound in characterization, so realistic in scene and thought, that one might boldly label its author a semi-Ibsenist, did he not exhibit a poetical charm, a splendour of dark tinting, above all, a richness of atmosphere, which sunder him utterly from every other dramatist of our day. Unfortunately he does, in fact, stand alone at present in this enthralling type of work wherein intellect is not clouded, but illuminated, by emotional sympathy and poetical imagination; for Mr. Barker, who gave distinct signs of it in *Ann Leete*, has passed over to a post-Ibsenist manner.

Thus at last we come to the authors whom I have put into a third section—Mr. Shaw, Mr. Barker, Mr. Galsworthy, St. John Hankin, and George Calderon. Each of these has special merits and faults, but there can be no doubt that they form a distinct body as compared with such writers as Pinero or Masefield. They are the English Ibsenists, the realist school. But before we discuss them separately, let us be clear as to what we mean by realism.

There are at least two sorts of reality. On the one hand are the facts of life and nature as we meet them every day; on the other are facts, not as we see them, but as they are.

There are (that is) two final ways of looking at phenomena : isolated, as an animal sees them; grouped, as the Divine Mind sees them, an organized whole. Between these extremes lies the view of that divine animal, Man. By the law of his intellect he groups things so that he may understand them, though he for ever groups them imperfectly. The more scientific a man's brain, the more he will systematize his knowledge of physical facts; he will understand more deeply and more widely, in some measure 'thinking God's thoughts after Him.' That is what is meant by Science. The more poetical a man's spirit, the more he will systematize his sympathy with emotional fact ; the passions and conduct of an individual will be viewed more and more as the symbol and expression of the Divine Spirit, expressing itself through all humanity. That is the soul of Art. It follows, then, that the artist never renders things as they appear to the incurious gaze. It cannot be said of him always that " he touched nothing that he did not adorn," but it is always true that he touches nothing that he does not alter. Set Watts to paint the portrait of an actress or an alderman, ask Keats to describe a nightingale's song,

Rodin to carve some trifle for the garden of the Tuileries. From each you receive more than you asked for—not the ware of a tradesman, but the touch of an unseen hand, the utterance of a voice hitherto unheard.

Therefore, if realism be a form of art, it is not the mere portrayal of isolated facts. If it were, how would a picture be better than a photograph, a lyric more moving than a newspaper report? The simple truth is, that while transcendental literature works at two removes from the lowest plane of reality, realistic literature is still one remove therefrom. The diviner art works more inevitably in general truths; the essences of emotion are its very drink; it speaks as if the daily isolated things were half-forgotten upon the dark earth. The other form of art works in generalities too, that it may more illuminatingly expound the common experiences which confront it. One artist ascends the mountain that he may dwell nearer heaven; the other, that he may more clearly discern his path across the earth—but he does not stand upon the plain so long as the artistic impulse is upon him. The maker even of a realistic play uses the so-called facts of life merely as raw material. Mr. Galsworthy, as surely as M. Maeterlinck, must select, alter, and combine, so that his work may be an organized artistic whole. His drama will not be a mere reflex of actual events, in which endless interruptions and irrelevancies obscure the lesson which he seeks to inculcate.

It will now be clear what is meant when the name " realist " is given to Shaw, Barker, Galsworthy, and others. There are three great processes of composition which we may distinguish in the work of any dramatist. The distinction is logical only, for the playwright carries on all three acts of creation simultaneously. These three are to be found in a realist writer quite as certainly as in any other; there is no omission of features vital to art. The great and only difference between the transcendentalist and the realist lies in the relative importance attached by them to each of the processes. First, there is a series of scenes from life, events, and conversations which may actually have happened. Secondly, this subject-matter is kneaded and shaped and carved; irrelevant things are left out; the significant events are made to grow out of one another in a significant manner; people are set in circumstances which throw just the right illumination upon their characters. Thirdly, the artist, as a master of language, adds the charm of directness and wit to his dialogue. This last is by no means superficial polish only. No writer but the merely clever persifleur, like Wilde, garnishes a bald situation with blazing but imported epigrams. For the supremely great author every word is a part of the plot. Let me take a few instances almost at random. On the first page of Mr. Thomas Hardy's most dramatic novel, we are told that the clergyman jestingly nicknamed an old peasant " Sir John." This tiny joke, like the breath of wind which dispatches an avalanche upon its career, is the starting-point of all that history of love and bloodshed which is called *Tess of the d'Urbervilles*. Shakespeare gives an amazingly skilful instance in that scene of *The Merchant of Venice* where Shylock entraps Antonio: his life must be in the bond, but how insert it without arousing fatal suspicions? The usurer, to defend his usury, quotes the story of Jacob and Laban's flocks. This puts the notion of Hebrews and flesh and usury into Antonio's head. Mark his own words :—

> When did friendship take
> A *breed* for barren metal of his friend ?

Thus, when the terms are mentioned, the shock of surprise, which would have wrecked the whole plot, is not felt. An equally vital instance occurs in *The Wild Duck*, where Gregers Werle directly causes the death of little Hedwig by his choice of a metaphor.

All these three processes or features, which one may briefly call photography, construction, and wit, are to be found as I said, in the English Ibsenists. It only needs to be added that there is perhaps an exaggeration of photography in most of their work. But, whatever their faults, they (with minor writers of their type) form the only school of British playwrights which practises dramatic art as distinguished from merely theatrical adroitness.

St. John Hankin produced seven plays: *The Two Mr. Wetherbys, The Return of the Prodigal, The Charity that began at Home, The Cassilis Engagement, The Last of the de Mullins,* and two one-act pieces, *The Burglar who failed* and *The Constant Lover.* I take this writer first because, though his work is chronologically more recent than that of the others, it is artistically earlier. Hankin is, indeed, an interesting study in transition. *The Two Mr. Wetherbys* has strong affinities with the Neo-British School. The exposure of the husband, through the discovery of a music-hall programme in his pocket, is only a symptom of this; and the feebleness and the staginess of all the characters, except the extraordinary Dick, is a weakness in execution, not in conception. But the theatrical triviality of the theme, above all the frantically absurd " happy ending " by which the devil-may-care husband belies his whole character and the trend of the whole play so that the curtain may descend as of old upon couples instead of units— these ghastlinesses mark the pre-Ibsenist born too late. The other works show a quite different tone. Even the first of them —*The Return of the Prodigal*—is so much more mature and certain in its handling that I cannot repel the suspicion that *The Two Mr. Wetherbys* is a youthful production brushed up for the stage a good many years after it was written. But *The Prodigal* evinces real observation and artistic sincerity. It is the story of a wastrel who really *is* a wastrel; he is not a "victim of circumstances" or "a rough diamond," or a good trusting fellow betrayed and badgered by his villainous rival through three acts, only to save the heroine from a burning mill in the fourth. No; he is by birth inefficient —a gentleman, good-natured, and discreet, but material prosperity flees from his most crafty stalking. There are such people, and Hankin gives us a first-rate study of one of them, a study both amusing and pathetic, unmarred by a cowardly "happy ending."

In *The Charity that began at Home* a lady decides to "do good" by inviting to her country-house people whom no one else will entertain. She thus gathers round her an extraordinary group of nuisances—an ogre of a governess who insists on poor Lady Denison learning *der die das* at the busiest hours of the day; a terribly common commercial traveller; a shady ex-lieutenant of "the Munsters"; a positively paralysing bore of an Anglo-Indian colonel of the "Poona-Horse-my-boy" type, and so forth. The discovery by these wretches of the reason Lady Denison had for inviting them makes an effective scene, but the play as a whole falls flat, because Hankin never made up his mind whether he intended comedy or mere farce. *The Cassilis Engagement* produces the same effect of amiability and weakness, though here the author is very successful in his country-house atmosphere. But the whole rests on a psychological impossibility. For a youth of the type represented by Geoffrey Cassilis to become engaged to a girl like Ethel Borridge is as near a miracle as a respectable Ibsenist can get. The dialogue, here as elsewhere, is admirable —a kind of compromise between the wit of Wilde and the wit of Shaw. We still feel the spirit of transition, another symptom of which is the exaggerated commonness of Ethel and her mother. It shows what Hankin thought of his audience: "They are so stupid and vulgar themselves that they won't see I mean these women as vulgar unless I make them positively gutter-bred." His best work is undoubtedly *The Last of the de Mullins*—the story of a girl who deliberately breaks loose from the benumbing life in a home ruled by faded memories of land-owning and lineage, in order to find life and interest. Cool and practical, but not impatient of her emotions, rather inspired by them, she is a curiously charming figure. The whole work has a tender richness and appeal. Both this and (still more) *The Prodigal* are Ibsenist, but at two removes, for they were clearly written under the influence of Shaw.

Mr. John Galsworthy shows the strongest contrast to Hankin. He seeks neither grace nor sublimity; his sole aim is reform. Moved to indignation by some social injustice he takes us by the scruff of the neck and forces us to stare at the horror. His hard, driving, doctrinaire manner is often terribly inartistic; but at least it makes for an athletic simplicity, a clear-cut structure. Yet he seems to forget a vital truth. One aim of the drama should be to entertain. I do not mean to amuse; I employ the word " entertain " because I cannot think of a better term for the effect of art : an austere but solid satisfaction, a quiet possession of one's soul, a refreshment of the emotions, which is the ministration of genuine tragedy as of genuine comedy. Mr. Galsworthy often seems too busy pommelling some special form of white-waistcoated iniquity to trouble about eternal truths. His less known and less effective plays are in this respect more successful. *The Eldest Son* conveys a certain grace of background—that atmosphere of a country-house which Mr. Galsworthy has so admirably given in his novels. *The Pigeon* is half-way between emotional drama, as in *The Eldest Son*, and the nagging admonitions of *Justice*. It contains good social satire and well-drawn types, especially an admirable Frenchman with at least one noble speech which clearly marks the writer's kinship with Shaw and Hankin. Ferrand is indeed the prodigal Eustace of Hankin, with less calculation but more alertness and profundity. The speech is Galsworthy's own expression—no other dramatist of our time could have penned it :—

Since I saw you, Monsieur, I have been in three institutions. They are palaces. One may eat upon the floor—though it is true—for kings—they eat too much of skilly there. One little thing they lack—those palaces. It is understanding of the 'uman heart. In them tame birds pluck wild birds naked . . . Oh! Monsieur, I am loafer, waster—what you like—for all that poverty is my only crime. If I were rich, should I not be veree original, 'ighly respected, with soul above commerce, travelling to see the world ? And that young girl, would she not be " that charming ladee," " veree chic, you know !" And the old Tims—good old-fashioned gentleman—drinking his liquor well. Eh! bien—what are we now? Dark beasts, despised by all.

The Silver Box (1906) is the earliest of the plays. A dissipated young man of fair position, and a dissipated young man of no position, both commit the same offence. Each steals something to spite some one whom he dislikes — the undergraduate a woman's reticule, the ex-groom a silver box. For the undergraduate everything is made easy by his father the M.P., by a discreet solicitor, and by the smooth negligences of the law. No one stands up for the ex-groom, and he goes to prison loudly protesting against the advantage given to his brother-offender by money and influence. Construction is given by the ex-groom's wife, who is a charwoman employed by the undergraduate's mother, and by the fact that the stolen box is the property of the undergraduate's father. The woman is accused of stealing the box. After denying the theft she goes home to find her husband in possession of the plunder. While she is reproaching him, they are surprised by a detective sent by the M.P. The third act is concerned entirely with the scene in a police court, where the sinister contrast between rich immunity and helpless poverty is demonstrated with pungency. On the artistic side the play is very good. All the characters are alive, and work together admirably to produce dramatic effect. There is nothing exaggerated or strained; the collision in the last act is acute but quite naturally induced. The propagandist side of the drama does not fully concern us. It is, however, important to notice that Mr. Galsworthy entirely agrees with the comment of the unhappy Jones: " Call this justice ? What about 'im ? 'E got drunk! 'E took the purse—'E took the purse, but it's *'is money* got *'im* off! Justice!" With this he agrees, and his whole aim is to impress us with the contention that men are *not* equal before the law. It is not his contention, but his method of handling it, with which we are concerned, and to which we shall return.

Justice is more simple in outline—a plain heart-rending story of a weak young man who, to save the woman he loves from a brutal husband, determines to leave the country with her, and for this purpose swindles his employers. The fraud is discovered before he escapes; the result is prison for three years and the utter ruin of his life and of the woman's. The whole second act is filled by an elaborate law-court scene, where Mr. Galsworthy's doctrinaire manner reaches its apotheosis in an extraordinarily long speech by the counsel for the defence, in which (here is the vital point) the view taken by the playwright himself is given with complete exactness as well as eloquence. On the stage it must take pretty nearly ten minutes to deliver—a portentous length. But Mr. Galsworthy intends to give the public, not what it wants or thinks it wants, but what it ought to want. The speech is not excused by beauty or surprising strokes, like numberless orations in Shakespeare. It has nothing but a direct and simple vigour. "In those four minutes the boy before you has slipped through a door, hardly opened, into that great cage which never again quite lets a man go—the cage of the Law."

The third and fourth acts depict photographically the prison life of this youth, and the maimed creature who at length comes forth with a ticket-of-leave. He cannot keep employment, he has to forge references, he does not report himself to the police; they come for him again, and he escapes only by instant suicide. In artistry *Justice* is the extreme case of photographic work, and must take low rank. As a piece of propagandism it is most effective.

On these two plays the present dramatic reputation of Mr. Galsworthy chiefly rests, for his recent *Skin Game* recalls *The Eldest Son* without equalling it; the atmosphere is admirably conveyed, but the dramatic tone is that of diluted melodrama. He is far too much of a pamphleteer and too little of a poet. Mr. Galsworthy's social sense, his burning zeal for righteousness in the State, command respect and emulation. And every citizen has a right—it is his duty—where he thinks institutions cruel and wasteful, to protest with all his strength. And he may make his novel, even his tragedy, a vehicle for such protests. But it is vital beyond words that he should beware *how* he makes his appeal. Never must he deliver a definite attack upon a definite abuse. If he does, his success may be tremendous at the moment, but it is dearly bought. He will always be remembered as a partisan; and his next pronouncement will be viewed, by all except those convinced by his first, with a potential hostility fatal to the appreciation of art. They will be alert, but with the wrong kind of alertness; the really eternal things he has to say have been terribly discounted beforehand. No; our prophet of the stage must alter, not the catchwords of the hour, not the policy of this year, but the human heart, the attitude of mind from which these policies spring and over which such catchwords exercise their dominion. He must so speak and teach that the foolish opinion becomes, not merely discredited, but impossible.

We turn now to Mr. Granville Barker, who has deserved better of the English theatre than any man living. As actor, as manager, as producer, as playwright, he stands in the foremost rank; he is also one of the chief agitators for a National Theatre. His plays are *The Marrying of Ann Leete, The Voysey Inheritance, Waste, The Madras House,* and *Prunella,* the last being written in conjunction with Mr. Laurence Housman. *Prunella* is not drama at all, but a sort of fairy fantasy; it is with the others, the realistic dramas, that we are now concerned.

Ann Leete is a picture of upper-class life in the eighteenth century. A young girl, daughter of a soulless politician, is to be married in order to further his party schemes. She learns to see through him and her suitor. Before her eyes, moreover, is her elder sister, who has been sacrificed in the same way and is now to be divorced because her father has deserted her husband's party. Suddenly Ann throws the whole sordid system over and asks the gardener to marry her; she will rather have the first man she sees, provided he is honest and healthy. The play concludes with the only beautiful scene in Mr. Barker's dramas, the home-coming of the strange couple to their poor little cottage.

Many have thought that *Ann Leete* is a different type of play from the rest, deceived by the simple charm of the close and by the eighteenth-century garnishing of post-chaises, duels, Brighton, and the like. Really it is much the same; the burden of the whole is: "Away with shams! We don't even know what we want. Let us find out, and do it." Still, there is in this first of Mr. Barker's works a touch of archaic beauty, in virtue of which *Ann Leete* claims affinity with *Prunella* as well as with *Waste*.

The Voysey Inheritance depicts a legacy of dishonour. A young solicitor, admitted into partnership by his father, discovers something wrong in the administration of certain trusts. On investigation he finds that his father has for many years been guilty of shady manipulations. Instructed to invest money at a low and safe percentage, he has speculated in high, dangerous percentages, paying the correct dividends out of his gains. This was done in the first instance to get the firm out of difficulties. When the dangers were past, the buccaneering instinct prompted him to begin again; it has not only created his income but added zest to the grey decorum of a solicitor's career. The father, after detailing all this in a curiously clever gospel of immorality, duly dies, and Edward Voysey is at the head of affairs, which are now in a bad state. His first idea is to proclaim everything and take the consequences. But he cannot bear to ruin the small investors, and determines to save some of them first. This he can only do by continuing his father's tactics; he works on, expecting exposure day by day. Soon an old friend of the father, who has no confidence in the son, announces that he wishes to withdraw his own large investments from the firm. This precipitates matters. He is told the facts, but is bought off (for the sake of the poor clients) by a promise of repayment. The end is a picture of young Voysey settling down to a life of toil in order to repair his father's ravages.

Waste is another simply-conceived story—that of a young statesman, Henry Trebell, a genius who has the originality to conceive great schemes of reform, the talent necessary to organize them, and the tenacity required for achievement. His ruin, and the wreck of all his glorious plans, springs from a moment's madness in which he becomes entangled with a married woman, a passionately egotistical but otherwise entirely null person. The result of this liaison is depicted with unflinching candour. Mrs. O'Connell, unknown to Trebell, undergoes an illegal operation, which kills her. All this becomes known, and his colleagues find it necessary to throw Trebell over. The tragic fact, that a pretty shell of a woman can ruin real work and genuine hopes, is here depicted with splendid skill and verisimilitude.

The Madras House is less strong, but more complicated and varied. There is no real plot, or rather the formal plot is strangely sundered from the genuine interest of the play; it recounts merely the sale of a great costume business to a commercial but romantic American. On this peg is hung a magnificent fabric of discussion, mainly about the social position of women. Female assistants in large shops, the living-in system, the life of the normal married woman in England, the effect on men's work of the presence and co-operation of women—these topics are handled with brilliant originality and fluent eloquence. The study is made dramatic by the contrast between Henry Huxtable and his partner Constantine Madras. Huxtable is positively steeped in home affections and Victorian stolidities; one feels that he could not be happy in Heaven without antimacassars and a marble clock. Madras is elaborately contrasted with him at every point. Not only has he so revolted against English home life that he has deserted his wife and son many years ago; Mr. Barker, in order to provide the external point of view, has actually converted him to Mohammedanism, and conferred upon him a house and harem in an Arabian village. This person's comments on the Englishman's attitude towards women are both novel and deadly, provoking a healthy reaction or commanding revolution. The upshot is that women are a disturbing and destructive factor in the ordinary business of the world; confined to the house in the Eastern fashion, they would perform their function of brightening life and soothing the wearied soul. We thus arrive, by another road, at the same conclusion as that to be derived from *Waste*.

In describing the plots of these plays, I have omitted what appears to many their strongest feature. It is a significant comment on Mr. Barker's art that I could so omit them. In all the four he has devoted remarkable skill to depicting a number of people, usually members of one family, whom he distinguishes from one another by the subtlety of his character-drawing. The instance of the Voysey family is celebrated. They swarm over the stage—the swindling father; the placidly deaf mother; the rather priggish son, Edward (the hero); the eldest son Trenchard, a clever and callous barrister; other sons, Booth Voysey the absurd domestic bully, and Hugh the artist; then daughters, a daughter's *fiancé*, a son's *fiancée* and sons' wives. There was a premonition of this *tour de force* in the Leete family, which in the third act holds a kind of review of these household troops. In *Waste* the politicians and their equally political wives and sisters interweave themselves in an ingenious but confusing pattern. Mr. Barker has received great praise—deserved praise—for this virtuosity, and seems to recognize in it his special *métier*. At any rate he reaches the climax in the first act of *The Madras House*, where he hurls at one's head no less than six daughters of the Huxtable line, all alike as lead pencils after some weeks' use (as he says himself), differing only in length, sharpening, and wear. This first act is a mist of daughters, who circle round their goaded parent like matadors round a Spanish bull.

All this, of course, is so much photography, like a great deal of Mr. Wells' work. Both Mr. Wells and Mr. Barker have been much lauded for it, and with little discrimination. Such descriptions are only the raw material of a novel or a play. If a man makes it an integral part of his completed work, he is not necessarily to be praised for doing so, any more than a cook is to be eulogized because she has chosen the proper ingredients; the proof of the pudding is not entirely in her good intentions. If anyone will compare the photograph work of *Love and Mr. Lewisham* with that of *The Return of the Native* he will appreciate this distinction.

Now, Mr. Barker's observation produces admirable work—let that be heartily granted. The question is, how does he employ these photographs? His intention, of course, is to give atmosphere, in which we can sympathize with the actors and understand the bearings of the drama. And it generally is thus useful. In *Ann Leete* the family tree bears little dramatic fruit; it seems to have been shown merely to interest the audience in the elaborate entanglement of aunts and sons-in-law—it would not be missed from the genuine action. *The Voysey Inheritance* marks a definite advance. Old Voysey shows up far better at home ensconced in this jungle of relatives. Still more to the purpose is the fact that we can see the kind of people young Edward has to deal with, in his attempt to put things right at all costs to his family. Even so, however, great masses of the dialogue are only first-rate padding, especially the delightful Major, whose personality is that of a strenuous blue-bottle. The statesmen and political ladies of *Waste* show a further improvement. Carefully studied for their own sakes, they are more germane to the action than the Voyseys. It is essential that Trebell should be understood in contrast with the more ordinary types of legislator; and Mr. Barker does give us a valuable background, the governing-class atmosphere, with extraordinary skill. Finally, in *The Madras House* this aspect is more dramatic again. If we are to study domesticity, it is essential to give an elaborately clear picture of one man's home life.

This dramatist's writings exhibit a second characteristic of even greater moment—the set discussion. I do not, of course, mean only the working out of a situation by talk. Every dramatist above the mask-and-revolver level practises that. I refer to the habit of set debate, discussion almost as elaborate and self-conscious as in a debating club. It is herein that Mr. Barker is most advanced—I will not commit myself to saying towards what he has advanced; but he has certainly gone beyond Ibsen. In this regard *Ann Leete* does show an authentic difference from the later plays; there is no debate at all. But *The Voysey Inheritance* has a good deal of it. *The Madras House* has more, and it is not vital to the plot. *Waste* is a positive portent from the present point of view. Trebell is talking all the time, and he talks like a Blue-book drastically revised by a wary archangel. Around him is a whole galaxy of lesser talkers, all mouthpieces for various opinions. The only fine creation is Amy O'Connell, but she is magnificently drawn.

The most distinguished member of this school is Mr. Bernard Shaw; among the writers whom we are discussing he is not only the most brilliant, he is the most like Ibsen. In his evidence before the Commission on the Censorship he remarked that his special work was the composition of immoral plays. This boast is the clue to his art as it is to that of his Norwegian predecessor. Realizing the waste that comes from a blind adoration of the *status quo*, he insists on revising current conventions; if anything has been unquestioned for more than a dozen years it is in his eyes open to the worst suspicion. Mr. Shaw's method is to take a romantic situation, dear to the unreal stage of pre-Ibsen days, and to develop that situation in his own way—a way novel, and therefore literally shocking, to the unwary spectator, but (as its author claims) thoroughly true to life. Thus *The Devil's Disciple* contains the melodramatic conception of a wastrel who takes a good man's place at the gallows, and so saves him for his wife and his work. Now, beyond all question, the seasoned playgoer expects two things. One is a mass of heroics about self-sacrifice. Anyone could write them: " I've been the devil's disciple throughout my life; but, by Heaven, in my death I'll serve something or Some One higher than that!" But the Shavian leopard cannot change its spots; Dick Dudgeon merely explains that when the soldiers came for the minister and arrested himself by mistake, though one word would have taken the noose from his own neck and put it round another man's, he found he simply could not utter it. The other feature that was inevitable a few years ago is a sudden love for the minister's wife springing up in Dudgeon's heart at the critical hour: " Yes, I love her! And how could my love show itself more nobly than by saving her husband at the cost of my own worthless life? And she shall—never—know!" Nothing of the kind. He has little interest in the lady, but he cannot save himself at the expense of an absent man—that is all. At this point should be related a most exasperating but laughable proof of the strength of tradition. When *The Devil's Disciple* was first produced, its author was out of England. The part of Dick Dudgeon was acted by no less an artist than Sir Johnston Forbes-Robertson. Now, in spite of the obvious trend of the action, the spirit of the play, the very words of the dialogue, the actor was so steeped in theatrical tradition that, in the midst of his colloquy with the minister's wife, he surreptitiously lifted a curl of her hair and kissed it. Could anything show more plainly through what a mass of dead convention the new drama has to dig its way?

Of this anti-romantic method *Cæsar and Cleopatra*, in spite of its gorgeous setting and august personages, is in all essentials another example. The mightiest Julius is here little more than the Shavian spirit wearing a breastplate and similar trappings; I hasten to add that he is delightful beyond words—one of the most virile, fresh, gripping personalities in literature. He passes through the play, the incarnation of inspired common-sense, pricking mercilessly the bubbles of vanity, sham ideals, and hypocrisy, sparing neither others nor himself. An opportunist in detail, he has a genuine ideal, peace and sane government for the Roman world.

Mr. Shaw's most recent plays are *Heartbreak House* and *Back to Methuselah*. The former claims to present in the manner of (*e.g.*) Tchekof the chaotic state of contemporary English society and ideas; its technique is clever, but no less chaotic than its theme. *Back to Methuselah* consists of a preface and five short plays depicting and discussing the necessity to extend indefinitely the length of human life. In this work Mr. Shaw passes practically outside the purview of dramatic criticism. On the one hand, these five "parts" are (strictly speaking) not plays at all, but static presentations of phases in the history of Man's relation to the conditions of his life. But, on the other hand, Mr. Shaw has not tried to write drama at all, in the ordinary sense. His prefaces have always been important;

but here the preface is the main part of the book, while the plays are merely long appendices. He puts forward a history of biological theory and develops therefrom a sketch of what he regards as the sound scientific religion of the future. Man must evolve the power to live for an indefinitely long period, because only so can he fulfil the purpose of the Life-Force. All this is set forth with an erudition, a philosophic vigour and breadth of comprehension, which awake the liveliest admiration and gratitude. Beside this preface the plays themselves are like the performances wherewith school-children are encouraged to realize the greatness of Alfred or Cromwell.

For several reasons we must not attempt a complete survey of Mr. Shaw's work. Let us merely note certain dominant facts. One point that he presses ruthlessly upon us is the importance of instinct. We saw how Richard Dudgeon's "heroism" was analysed as neither cynicism nor divinity, but blind impulse. So too in *Blanco Posnet* the abandoned scoundrel acts like a courageous gentleman, and curses himself afterwards for doing so; instinct forces him to risk his life by surrendering his horse to the lone woman and her sick child. Major Barbara has an instinct for saving men from themselves which survives even the collapse of what she thought most fundamental in her life. In *Androcles and the Lion* we observe the same power of impulse ; none of the martyrs, different in type as they are, acts from deliberate valour or calculation or even clearly understood religious belief. Lavinia can give no reason for her sacrifice of life ; Ferrovius flings away his crown of glory because war is in his veins; and the wretched Spintho, who seeks martyrdom that his rascally life may be followed by eternal joy, flings away his scheme at the last moment—through instinct again.

It is on these lines that Mr. Shaw studies love between the sexes, a subject to which, more than any other, he has devoted his rare psychological insight and sincerity of expression. *Man and Superman* contains the fullest account of his theory. In the first place, love has nothing to do with intellect, compatibility, wisdom, public spirit, perception of beauty or of noble character ; it is simply Nature (instinct again, the instinct of the Universe) which throws two people into one another's arms. And secondly, it is the woman who woos, the man who is won; the woman who pursues, the man who — runs away, to be blunt. In this view it must be owned that Shaw has support from two great authors who certainly never heard of Ibsen; namely Shakespeare and Dickens. The Gloria and Valentine of *You never can Tell* are trembling combatants in this duel of sex; more hardy fighters are Charteris and Julia in *The Philanderers*; *Widowers' Houses* presents the same type, but of commoner grain, in Harry Trench and Blanche Sartorius; similar, in a more delicate and repressed manner, are Major Barbara and Cusins; the same conflict, more poignant perhaps than ever, thrills through *John Bull's Other Island*. *Getting Married* is no duel of this kind; it is a general engagement, horse, foot, and guns, between four men and four women. But *Man and Superman* is the most elaborate presentation, and with finely dramatic audacity it includes an actual flight of the man, breaking records indeed in his motor-car, but nevertheless overtaken on his way to a Mohammedan country where, as he says, men are protected from women.

This great play leads us on to the next topic—Mr. Shaw's ability and usefulness as a constructive thinker. For the third act, the famous dream sometimes separately played under the title *Don Juan in Hell*, is at once the most highly-wrought instance of the dramatic discussion above referred to, and an apparently complete pronouncement of the writer's positive philosophy. As argumentative eloquence it is one of the glories of English literature; as a gospel it is a lugubrious failure. The high mission of Man is to carry on the will of the Universe; Heaven is a state in which his efforts to understand that will are to be unclouded by the preoccupations of the flesh. But what the will of the world is we are not told, and the goal of Man is—to go on striving towards a goal, the latter goal being apparently unknown. This is but a vague boon in place of an orthodox Heaven, just as Mr. Shaw's much adored Life-Force is an unsatisfactory substitute for a personal Deity. There is in this, however, little to disturb us, unless we are to demand perfection from our leaders. Shaw is not a builder, but a destroyer. To create a new world is noble and necessary; it is equally necessary and little less noble to clear the ground of whatever false creeds and sham civilizations encumber it.

More than any other, Mr. Shaw is a master of the dramatic epigram. In sheer brilliance, amazing as he is, Congreve and Wilde perhaps surpass him; but there is an immense distinction to be made. Congreve and Wilde seem to have written plays for the sake of working off epigrams. Shaw uses his wit to point the play. Wilde's epigrams are fireworks; Shaw's are beacons. What could be better than this from *Candida* ?

MORELL: Eugene, my boy: you are making a fool of yourself. There's a piece of wholesome plain speaking for you.

MARCHBANKS: Oh, do you think I don't know all that ? Do you think that the things people make fools of themselves about are any less real and true than the things they behave sensibly about ?

This is more than clever. It is an astounding illumination to almost every one who hears it for the first time, both amusing him and teaching him wisdom. Still more, it reveals the secret of Eugene's terrible power—that of a naked soul whose weapon is an indifference to the ready grin of the crowd at the man who does not hide his feelings. Through this power he reveals the real woman behind Miss Garnett's brassy respectability, the inmost soul of the superficially benevolent Candida, the unsuspected weakness of Morell the clergyman. So with Larry Doyle's comparison of an Englishman to a caterpillar in the first act of *John Bull's Other Island* : the caterpillar makes himself look like a leaf so that the birds may overlook him, while he devours the real leaves; so does the Englishman pretend to be a fool that clever people may not meddle with him while he eats up all the real fools. This makes us laugh at the time, and it is the quintessence of all the rest of the play. Broadbent wins a seat in Parliament and a wife by his apparently whole-hearted idiocy.

Let us finally point to one more dramatist, the lamented George Calderon, whose *Fountain* is a play of extraordinary merit. Prefixed to it is a little jewel of a preface in which Mr. Calderon repudiates the charge (or eulogium) of Shavianism; he claims to have expressed " a truth which never entered the Shavian head." This truth is hinted at in the motto (taken from Longfellow, of all pre-Ibsenists under the sun !) : " That which the fountain sends forth returns again to the fountain."

The play deals with slum-work. A

spirited girl goes to live among the poor and thriftless. She does all she can to cheer and help them, even instituting a pawnshop of a most unbusinesslike kind. Then, finding (naturally enough) that she has too little money, she asks her solicitors to improve her investments. They refuse. She changes her solicitors, gets more money for her work, but is daunted to hear almost at the same time that the rents of her flock have been raised. And so the thing goes on, the exactions of the slum-landlord keeping pace with her endeavours to aid the poor. Her rage against the oppressor grows almost hourly, till she finds by accident that the landlord is herself, and the increase of funds for social work has been obtained by rackrenting the objects of her charity. The whole thing is written with strength and ingenious simplicity. The dialogue is charmingly crisp and witty, the atmosphere rich and convincing. Of all modern English plays it is the only one not by Mr. Shaw which is comparable to Mr. Shaw's best work.

If I am to sum up my view of the English Ibsenists, it is this. Hankin is a blend of the old stagey school represented by Pinero, of Ibsenism as expounded in England by

Shaw, and of the superficial society-comedy cultivated by Wilde. Mr. Galsworthy is a propagandist who uses his "sense of the theatre" and his perception of psychology too often as an engine of controversy. Mr. Barker is almost as much of a pamphleteer, but also more of an artist. A little insistent and shrill, he has carried the Ibsen manner into new and dubious developments. Mr. Shaw is a great artist, a superb wit, and a preacher of doctrines too often unsatisfying even when they are satisfactory. Calderon is a Shavian with no Shavian shibboleths. Of the school as a whole it may be said that they are good workmen, overrated as apostles and decried as charlatans. Hankin, Barker, and Galsworthy are good dramatists in the sense in which the man who made this writing-table was a good workman; but he was not a Hepplewhite or a Sheraton, neither are they Ibsens. There are two reasons for the unduly high praise given to these playwrights by many excellent critics. Firstly, they deserve great attention, if not applause, for the opinions which they hold and expound. But this has nothing in the world to do with their merits as playwrights. (It is neglect of this obvious distinction, by the bye, which has caused Mr. Shaw to lavish amazing eulogies upon that third-rate writer, Brieux.) Secondly, they do their work sincerely and well, and English playgoers compare them, not with Ibsen, but with their English predecessors and contemporaries. When Robinson Crusoe, after many years spent in conversation with a solitary parrot, found a companion in Man Friday, he did not at once complain of his primitive costume or his taste in the arts. Nor does the cultivated playgoer pick holes in *The Voysey Inheritance* or *The Return of the Prodigal* after the lucubrations of Robertson, Marston, and their kin. Nevertheless our present leaders are mostly but good second-rate writers if viewed by really high standards. Mr. Shaw is undoubtedly above this level, but it is legitimate to conjecture that his best achievement lies behind him.

A splendid feature of this renaissance is the rise of repertory theatres in Birmingham, Glasgow, Dublin, and elsewhere. These are a welcome sign that the provinces are beginning to escape from the real blight of provincialism—that humble waiting on London for the scraps of inferior bread which she chooses to fling. Even now, for the majority of our people the discussion set up in this essay is an academic discussion only; the Renaissance of English Drama passes us by, unless we have a taste for reading plays or are able to visit London. Many an English city, renowned to the ends of the earth for its commerce and material enterprise, is content to see in its theatre from year's end to year's end nothing better than loose French farces produced at second-hand, or miserably empty and derivative English pieces sent on "the road" as "London successes." But of late, as we said, there are signs, not only of renewed life in the drama itself, but in the popular feeling about that form of art. The high cost of travel and other difficulties are compelling provincial towns to forgo the work sent down from London, and willy-nilly to foster local amateur enterprise. To exchange the ordinary revue, presented by jaded third-rate professionals, for *Twelfth Night* or *The Silver Box*, presented by enthusiastic amateurs, is an immense reform. We may yet see dramatic art once more a function of the national culture.

THE NATURE AND METHODS OF DRAMA

DESPITE the vast accumulation of written and oral criticism which has been devoted to particular plays, to acting and stage management, to the types of drama, and to drama itself as distinguished from other forms of art, there is room, and even demand, for a plain and comparatively brief statement setting forth the principles on which all sound dramatic work is constructed. Anyone who attempts such a statement must be fearlessly dogmatic: detailed reservations and periodical expressions of self-distrust, though manifestly required in an elaborate disquisition, would impair the usefulness of a mere introduction to the subject. This dogmatic method can mislead no one; the alleged facts are derived from induction, and the reader from moment to moment may test them by reference to any play which he thinks fit to select. Considerations of space have made it necessary to omit all save quite necessary allusions to well-known theories.

"Drama" is a Greek word meaning "action," "thing done," and it might therefore be supposed that a play is merely the reproduction, by imitation, of some act or series of acts. Not so; the name points to the artistic medium, not the thing presented and as presented. All that it implies is that the artist uses, not pigments or musical notes, but speaking and moving human beings, as his raw material. An imitation by real people of such an event as Cæsar's landing in Britain, or the sealing of Magna Charta, is by no means necessarily dramatic, however exciting the spectacle, however important the event portrayed. It may be theatrical—that is, it may, by exaggerated gestures, tones, and language, amid a skilful setting, convey an impression of momentousness; but theatricality and drama are not the same thing. A true definition can be gathered only from the achievement of those whom the world in general has agreed to look upon as good dramatists.

What, then, is that feature, or what are those features, which all plays exhibit?

One element, and no other, is invariably present: a difficulty appropriately solved. Drama is the presentation by living persons of a complication in life and of the unravelling as effected by their interplay. It is not merely mimic action, but mimic action governed by a "plot." At the close of the first stage—in a modern play the first Act—some quite definite question, with all its difficulties realized, must be placed before us and awaken our urgent interest. It may refer to the broadest hopes or fears of humanity—Whither will Faust's titanic ambition lead him? How will Hamlet face the duty laid upon him by his father's spirit? Or it may be narrow, even trivial, though attractive — Which man will the heroine marry? Will the dispatches reach Grant in safety? After reading or witnessing the first Act we should be able to express in one sentence, yet completely, the question of the play. Some difficulty, puzzle, problem, or mystery is as essential to a drama as sap to a tree. Without it, no magnificence in the characterization of Hamlet or Faust, no charm or wit of the heroine, no historical colour or life-like portrayal of American generals, can make the work into a drama. The interlude of Mak in the Miracle-Play is as truly dramatic, though it deals but with the detection of a sheep-stealer, as is *Agamemnon* or *Macbeth*. For whatever mimic performance has plot is drama, and whatever lacks plot is not drama, no matter how admirable its mounting, its dialogue, its psychology. Just as *Robinson Crusoe*,[1] for all its interest and power, is no novel, since it has no plot, but is to be called a tale, so *Henry the Sixth* is no series of plays, but a chronicle.

The instance of *Robinson Crusoe* may help us to greater precision of thought. Is it true that there is no question or puzzle in the book's early stages? Do we not wonder how the hero will escape from his island-prison, and even more what kind of existence he will evolve for himself in his years of solitude? Is not this, then, a plot? And do we not meet with a solution? True;

[1] The first draft of this essay was written before I read Mr. William Archer's *Playmaking*, and I am interested to observe that he remarks (p. 25): "If we want to see will struggling against obstacles, the classic to turn to is not *Hamlet*, not *Lear*, but *Robinson Crusoe*; yet no one, except a pantomime librettist, ever saw a drama in Defoe's narrative." If the reader chances not to know Mr. Archer's book, I take this opportunity of recommending it enthusiastically for its learning, skill, lucidity, and artistic common sense.

we may ask ourselves these questions—we are certain to do so if we are really interested. But here is the vital point: the question does not *form the substance* of the action; it is only the natural outcome thereof in our own minds. The substance of the action is a series of interesting events: his shipwreck, his despoiling of the stranded vessel, his discovery of a footprint or a dying goat, his illness, and the like. It is not the fact that the earlier part of the story is unified and organized by its formulating in action some difficulty which we necessarily look to see surmounted, some problem the unguessed answer to which we confidently await. Contrast with this the early scenes of some play. Whereas Defoe gives us a mere succession of events, having no vital connexion, joined together only by the fact that they all concern the same man, in a drama the successive happenings are woven together into an organism. Each scene is interesting and clear in itself, but it also gains and bestows value through its juxtaposition with others. Omit Crusoe's parcelling of his gunpowder, and we do no harm to any other episode. But omit Macbeth's first meeting with the " weird sisters," or even the scene of the " bloody sergeant," and we lose something not only excellent in itself, but of plain importance to our appreciation of the murder-scenes and the final combat, indeed of the whole play.

What has been said so far relates to the question-part of the drama; but analogous remarks might be made about the answer-part, the *dénouement* or " untying of the knot." The answer or solution must be evolved by the interaction of the characters —the later scenes must be observed to come out of the earlier; to come out, not necessarily to grow out, for we are talking at present of drama in the widest sense. In a good play the solution will arise organically out of the question itself; in coarse drama it may merely leap out surprisingly. The answer may depend wholly on some hitherto unguessed revelation that the heroine is the villain's daughter. That would be poor drama; but bad drama is still drama. In a first-rate play the whole solution is inherent in the terms of the problem, though no spectator has the subtlety and wisdom fully to foresee it. But more will be said later on this important topic.

Other features of a playwright's work are

momentous, but there is none which stands on the same plane as structure, or plot.[1] All drama by its nature must have that; the others can be dispensed with, and often are dispensed with, in certain types of play. It therefore becomes necessary at this point to distinguish the various forms of dramatic art.

There are four chief types. The dramatist has always, as we saw, to deal with some tangle in human life, but his treatment will vary according to his philosophy of life and according to his temperament. The first factor will determine whether he shall portray life as serious or as absurd, there being of course arguments on both sides. The second factor determines whether his treat-

[1] This statement conflicts strongly with the marked trend of modern criticism in England. Professor Bradley's justly famous *Shakespearean Tragedy* deals far more with the psychology of Hamlet or Macbeth than with the structure of their plays. The same tendency is the main feature of Professor C. E. Vaughan's *Types of Tragic Drama*; and Mr. St. John Ervine, in an *Observer* of 1920, has asked, "What is the plot of *Hamlet*?" with the implication that the reply makes no matter. To deal with this wide topic adequately is impossible here. It can only be said (i) that the dictum offered above, like the whole essay, is based on consideration of drama ancient as well as modern; (ii) that plot is in Shakespeare, though highly important, yet less important on the whole than in Sophocles. Nevertheless, if one does detect the *peripeteia* of *Hamlet*—the death of Polonius—one finds even more interest in that masterpiece than before.

ment shall be profound or superficial. If a play presents the solemn view of life with depth, so that the action is clearly felt to typify the concerns of all humanity, the play is a tragedy. Its superficial counterpart is melodrama: there may be found in a melodrama as much sorrow, sin, and death as any tragic play contains, but our imagination (for whatever reason) is not led onwards and upwards from individual to universal concerns. So with the treatment which envisages the absurd. Comedy is drama that studies universal interests and depicts their meaning or influence, quite as certainly as does the tragic method, but it enlightens us through our sense of laughter, not of tears or horror. Its superficial counterpart is farce—the employment of the ludicrous to engage our attention in what does not touch our own heart or interests.

These four types one might perhaps expect on general grounds to approximate to one another. This does at times occur.[1] A tragedy may interest us more in the special instance than in the universal aspect raised

[1] So Mr. C. E. Montague in his delightful *Dramatic Values* (p. 27) mentions "the tang of grotesque tragedy which there is in many of the best farces and which helps to make *George Dandin* one of the best in the world."

by it; and in this way tragedy would merge into melodrama. There are, for example, a number of fairly good reasons for regarding even *Othello* as no less a melodrama than a tragedy. So with comedy and farce. The best " comic " scene in the whole range of letters—the passage in *Henry the Fourth* where Falstaff describes the Gadshill adventure—is as much farce as comedy. Still further, it is possible for tragedy and comedy themselves to merge into one another. The question here has, of course, nothing to do with tragi-comedy, which is nothing more than a play consisting of tragic scenes and comic scenes alternating. That is a " mechanical mixture ": what concerns us here is the possibility of a " chemical compound." Can a drama be both tragedy and comedy? Is it possible to treat a theme both seriously and laughably? On general grounds one would suppose the enterprise highly difficult but possible. Horace Walpole said that " Life is a comedy to those who think, a tragedy to those who feel "; therefore, given a playwright with a great brain and a great heart aiding, not thwarting, one another, such a drama is possible. To find a whole play composed in this godlike mood would be difficult, but scenes or whole acts written in that vein are well-known. *King Lear* owes its special and stupendous potency more perhaps to this than to any other single cause; and many a great passage in Euripides—parts of *Orestes*, for example—belongs to this category. The four great dramatic types, then, can and do at times approximate. But, as a fact, the centrifugal tendency has been far more strongly marked. Tragedy has grown more solemn and awful, melodrama more superficially wild, comedy more laughable, farce more vulgar, than in strict theory they need have become. Throughout large areas of dramatic history the conventions are secure that tragedy must culminate in the death of the chief personage, that comedy must not arouse thought, that melodrama should contain an unredeemed villain, that farce must exhibit horseplay with food, clothing, or furniture.

It has often been observed that good melodrama and good farce are rare; indeed "superior" people make a point of pretending that melodrama is actually funny because so "bad"—that is, because it bears no recognizable relation to life. This is to attribute to the whole class vices belonging only to feeble and stupid instances thereof; and it is easy to do so, because good melodrama is rare. But it exists—witness the *Helena* of Euripides, Kyd's *Spanish Tragedy,* perhaps even *Othello.* The reason for this rarity is that Man is a generalizing animal, so that both melodrama and farce, if well conceived and executed, might seem bound to become tragedy and comedy by leading the spectator from the special experiences before him to the facts of his own life and of humanity. This is not actually so; it is possible to compose both sorrowful and laughable drama, of admirable quality, which concerns only the people portrayed and not the whole race. Both types are saved by introducing features which necessarily and obviously pin down the interest to individuals. Farce is invariably distinguished from comedy by this feature, that the persons act, think, and speak lopsidedly—they ignore what could not be ignored in reality, and fasten upon some special, only minor, point, in the various situations, for example the muffins in *The Importance of Being Earnest.* Melodrama is invariably distinguished from tragedy by two qualities, theatricality and violence. There is no melodrama which does not depend in considerable degree upon stage tradition: every drama of this class is a more or less imposing structure built from the *débris* of tragic work. As for the other feature, all emotions are conveyed by crude and exaggerated physical action, on the most elaborate scale allowed by coarse sentimentalism and the resources of the theatre. Hatred may no doubt be evinced in tragedy by murder, but in melodrama the bloodshed must be wildly spectacular and complicated. In both types the same reason holds for these excesses; it is necessary to depart far enough from probability to prevent the spectator's identifying himself with the persons presented, yet not far enough to reach the unthinkable, for there interest would perish. Good melodrama and good farce, then, are rare because both must be unnatural yet interesting.

So necessary is it for us to follow only the main lines of this immense subject, that certain highly important considerations which will occur to the reader must be left on one side. There is, for instance, the curious fact that great comedy is rarer than great tragedy. Aristophanes is a mighty scenic genius, but his work often passes over from comedy to farce. Shakespeare has given us magnificent comic scenes, but no whole comedy which can be ranked with his greatest half-dozen tragedies. Molière is first-rate, and Marivaux full of delight; but it would be a mistake to put them on a level with Sophocles, however distinctly they surpass the tragic playwrights of their own country. Another attractive topic is the minor forms of drama: burlesque, which is farce pivoted upon parody; opera, which blends music with any one of the four main types already discussed; modern pantomimes and revues, which tend more and more to dispense with plot and so inevitably to lose dramatic quality and revert to chaos.

It is, however, desirable to offer some remarks on a kind of drama frequent in our own time. There are many excellent works which may be thought to fall under none of our four categories. It may be said that they are not laughable, and therefore neither comedy nor farce; that they appeal strongly to the instincts, fears, or interests of all men, and are therefore not melodramatic; that they do not culminate in the death of the chief character, and so are not tragic

—moreover, they lack the pomp and awe which we associate with tragedy. What then are they ? It is usual to term them simply " plays " or—implying some indefinitely tense quality—" dramas " ; and critics more or less vaguely suggest or assert that they constitute a new type of dramatic work. We are here, as often in criticism, within sight of a dispute about mere nomenclature, but it is worth while to seek greater precision. Such works as those just mentioned are tragedies. They conform to the definition of tragedy given earlier, and our unreadiness to allow them that name is due to the natural, but in this regard excessive, influence upon our judgment of the greatest tragic achievements. It seems at first sight absurd to place *Mrs. Warren's Profession*, excellent as it is, in the same class with *Œdipus Coloneus, Faust,* and *Hamlet.* But this is not a question of classes of merit ; it is a question of classes of method. Any drama, indeed, must fall more or less definitely into one of our four classes, the only variations being blends thereof. A word should be added concerning the theory that the hero's death is a necessary ingredient of tragedy. A very large proportion of the noblest tragedies do, of course, exhibit this feature, for reasons which are too obvious to need mention. But the function of tragedy can always be carried out competently, and has sometimes been carried out sublimely, by a plot which dispenses with this device; *Œdipus Tyrannus* and *Medea* are examples.

So much, then, for the nature of drama. What is its aim? Is there any one purpose which we can attribute to every drama, every playwright, every school of dramatic writing, despite the great divergences which are to be remarked between school and school, dramatist and dramatist, even between different works of the same author? Is there nevertheless any one object in which they all agree, just as there was one characteristic of form, namely, the question-and-answer plot, in which we found them all to agree? The divergences are great. Greek tragedy and comedy were parts of religious ritual; Roman comedy is a light comment on contemporary manners; Roman tragedy (so far as we know it) was translation of Greek, or, if original, machine-made rhetoric; mediæval plays are a crude attempt to impress upon the unlearned the robust reality of Scriptural stories or the validity of ethical dogma; modern dramas, when serious, deal with difficulties of conduct or social anomalies; when frivolous, they play superficially or deleteriously with the common emotions. Differences as great are apparent between dramatist and dramatist. The chief aim of Shakespeare is to edify through a study of emotion; of Sophocles, to reconcile Man with his environment through the appreciation of human instincts; of Ibsen, to fortify through a new appeal to ethical fact. Can we point to any common purpose or purposes? There is but one—to entertain, by the portrayal of life. This kind of entertainment—that is, the refreshment and invigoration of the intellect and emotions by depicting a human crisis and its solution—is common to *Œdipus Tyrannus*, to *Othello*, to *Tartuffe*, to *The Importance of Being Earnest*, and to the most dull, derivative, or vulgar piece ever concocted in Rome or mid-nineteenth-century England. It is said that the object of all art is to give pleasure by imitation. This dictum, though by no means completely untrue, is misleading; for no one with a sense of accuracy would give the name of "art" to a reproduction of creaking cartwheels or even of the nightingale's song, since art must always pass beyond simple mimicry, through reticence, frugality, and the blending touch of a human creator bringing forth what is not the familiar reproduced but the familiar transfigured. The aim of all art, then, is to give pleasure, not by mere imitation, but by reinforced reminiscence, and the aim of dramatic art is to give pleasure by the reinforced reminiscence of the critical in human life. True, the playwright often has a further purpose, some special thesis about conduct or emotion, as had De Musset in *On ne badine pas avec l'amour,* or some quite definite social doctrine for which he seeks converts, like Mr. Galsworthy in *Justice,* and above all, M. Brieux in *Les Avariés* or *Les Trois Filles de M. Dupont.* He may, that is, be a pure artist, presenting life as he sees it, with no plainly implied comment at all, or he may be a thoroughly didactic propagandist using dramatic method merely as a platform, or he may be anything between these extremes. The distance between Sophocles and M. Brieux provides room for many grades, not only of literary excellence, but of didacticism also. And however openly propagandist a playwright may be, we shall always find that he provides "entertainment"—the bracing and refreshment of mind and heart—in however attenuated a degree: there are always, at the least, piquant contrasts and a vivacity of dialogue which no mere pamphlet ever provides. But though such "entertainment" is always present, it is in some modern work painfully meagre; and herein lies some foundation for that watchword of the "Philistine" which so annoys lovers of the drama—"I go to the theatre to be amused." No doubt a series of guffaws extended over three hours is an experience not only unnecessary, but intolerable, to any civilized being not jaded by perverse and monotonous toil; and drama, like the other arts, aims at illuminating people whose minds are alert, whose taste is critical, not to provide opportunities for emotional dram-drinking. Nevertheless, the "Philistine" has his glance turned in the right direction; he is justified in his suspicion of performances which promise pleasure and betray him with sermons or social programmes.

The rest of this essay will deal with the methods of drama—the system of composition, the specific devices, whereby a playwright seeks to effect the purpose we have described; namely, to refresh and brace his hearer's intellect and emotions by portrayal of some puzzle in life and of its solution. His task must be carried out through his personages — that is, mainly by their characters, their actions, and their words: what they *do*. He may also employ external happenings: what is *done to them*. It will be convenient to examine this latter element first.

By "external happenings" are here meant things of which the characters must take account, but which arise without their volition, events of which we cannot say that they would naturally happen in the situation supposed, but only that they might happen at some time or other—a lightning-flash whereby the villain is removed, a violent shock which by restoring speech or memory makes of some negligible person an important witness, and so forth; most commonly of all, the use of coincidence to bring about meetings or discoveries.

Accidents, and structurally important accidents, are to be found in the greatest plays. Prospero's enemies are wrecked upon the one island, of all islands, where he himself was cast away.[1] Œdipus meets and slays the one man, of all men, who is his father. In *A Doll's House* Mrs. Linden and Krogstad meet by the merest chance, and on their meeting the celebrated final scene structurally depends. In lesser work, especially in melodrama and farce, such "external events" abound; many farces, indeed, almost consist of sudden confrontations, ludicrous but irrational. Accident should be sparingly employed in serious drama, because the author must present a recognizable picture of life, which depends, or is thought to depend (here the same thing), far more upon character than upon accident. It is accident that Romeo should fail to receive the Friar's letter and should enter the Capulets' vault before Juliet awakes; it is his character which causes him to destroy himself before her trance is broken. And when such accidents are employed, important distinctions must be

---

[1] The tempest itself is due to Prospero's art, but the fact that his enemies come within the focus of his power is the result of chance:—

> By accident most strange, bountiful Fortune—
> Now my dear lady—hath mine enemies
> Brought to this shore.

OF DRAMA

observed. It is bad dramatic art to set in the midst of the play a pure accident on which the subsequent action absolutely depends. For the spectator realizes that had the accident not occurred the story would have collapsed. It is no help to reply that vital accidents do appear in real life; art cannot be chaotic, and pure accident, to the human eye, is the incursion of chaos.

But we must note the wording: "to set in the midst of the play a pure accident on which the subsequent action absolutely depends." Two fundamental facts must be indicated here. First, there is by no means the same objection to such accident if it happens before the outset of the drama, or even at its opening. What starts the action may be illogical, casual, improbable, anything short of flat impossibility. One has to begin somewhere, and we do not object to an accident so long as the action itself, once opened, is logical and natural. One might as well censure Raphael's *School of Athens* on the ground that not all the philosophers there depicted could have come together, not being contemporaries. "Supposing they had been," the painter could reply, "that is how the assembly would have looked." Aristotle therefore rightly says that the irrational elements should be outside the play proper. It is this consideration which justifies two of the instances quoted above, those from *The Tempest* and *Œdipus Tyrannus*. The second point rests on the words " absolutely depends." It makes all the difference in the world whether the accident is one of action or of time only. In the first case the event itself is casual—that is, the chances are indefinite thousands to one against the event itself happening at all; and yet, if it did not, the subsequent action would vanish. An examination of Euripides' *Alcestis* will show that the *dénouement* depends, not upon Alcestis' devotion, or Admetus' anguish, or the valour of Heracles, but solely upon the fact that the demigod happens to become intoxicated; and unless we admit in *Alcestis* the notion so regular in comedy, that Heracles drinks too deeply whenever he has the opportunity, we must condemn Euripides' method in this drama. In most plays it is not the fact itself which is casual, but the time. The fact, or something like it, will certainly happen sooner or later: the only accident is that it should happen just then. On such accidents it is not true that the subsequent action "absolutely depends." Did not the event fall precisely when it does, we should not lose the later development, only quickness and precision of development; the drama in its outlines would be unchanged. This second consideration justifies the third example given above, from *A Doll's House*. It is on the one hand true that, had not Mrs. Linden and Krogstad met by pure chance in Helmer's drawing-room, Krogstad would not have spared Nora and her husband, therefore we should not have gained the great final scene as it stands. But the vital point is that that scene must necessarily arrive at some time, given Helmer's character and Nora's; all that the accidental meeting gives us is the neatness with which the last scene happens so early.

The other instrument, or set of instruments, with which a dramatist performs his task was, we saw, what the persons themselves do. This, in the widest interpretation, means their characters, their actions, and their words. Psychology, action, and dialogue are the three great strands of dramatic composition. Every play must exhibit them all, though their relative importance may vary: characterization must be effected by conduct and dialogue, action must reveal character and be clothed with conversation, dialogue must refer to character and the visible action of the piece.

Of these the most fundamental and most difficult is characterization. The question of the drama — the *desis* ("tying") as Aristotle calls it, the tangle, problem, or perplexity—should arise from the psychology of the persons involved, as well as from the situation in which they find themselves; this is equally, or even more, true of the *dénouement*. The specific pleasure afforded by dramatic art is to watch character creating destiny. It is true that a special situation is also needed, since a definite crisis must be raised by a definite cause. Among existing plays there are many gradations based on the relative importance of character and situation. In *Monsieur Piégois*, by M. Alfred Capus, the situation is merely that Piégois notices a lady who is travelling in the same railway compartment as himself. Works of heavier calibre begin more remarkably, since mighty crises are normally introduced by highly unusual events; both psychology and situation are wonderful in such works as *Agamemnon* and *Julius Cæsar*. Numberless feeble but violent productions, especially melodramas, show slight characterization and a tremendous or elaborate situation, such as Andreiev's *Sabine Women* and the pseudo-Shakespearean *Titus Andronicus*.

The means by which a dramatist may project a character are six: the things done by the person, the things said by him, the attitude of people who have been in close touch with him, things said of him by others, facts already known to the spectator, and material details. The last three may be used as subsidiary, but no one save an inferior workman relies on them; none the less, so arduous is it to create character effectively by the first three means, that many writers have depended perforce upon the cheaper and coarser devices.

Material details, such as the furnishing of a man's room or significant equipment of his person, are not really successful, save by convention. To fill an apartment with musical instruments and busts of Grieg or Mozart proclaims the occupant a musician —perhaps—but that is to tell us his hobby or trade, not his character. Dress a man in large checks and give him diamonds to wear; that proves his vulgarity—perhaps—but vulgarity is a matter of tone; it is colour, not structure; and character is the structure of the soul, while culture is its colour. Moreover, externals are as untrustworthy as obvious. The gaudily attired man may not be vulgar; he may hate these trappings and wear them to please his wife.

Another of these cheap devices was "facts already known to the spectator"—that is, the author evades his task by introducing some real person whose character is already known from history or legend. Let the curtain rise upon a short stout figure frowning into vacancy, wearing a cocked hat, and holding one hand thrust into his bosom, and the thing is done. He is Napoleon the Great, and every one in the theatre knows, not perhaps (or probably) his character, but those conventional characteristics which alone such a writer intends to exploit. The actor has but to snap his fingers and, without turning his head, exclaim: "Bernadotte, come here!" and the "character" is "created." It is to this simple method that the success of Mr. John Drinkwater's *Abraham Lincoln* is mainly due.

Analogous to this is the fourth expedient, "things said of him by others"—by far the greatest favourite of all. Just as second-rate dramatists open with elaborate unnatural explanations of the plot uttered by servants laying a dinner-table, so is character conveyed by a symposium of minor persons who have nothing better to do than diagnose their friend's or their master's private blend of irritability and a generous heart. When the person so described appears, he is not further characterized by more artistic means if the author is really second-rate; the fluid phantasma runs easily into the mould thus prepared. There is no strong objection to such preparation if the person described makes it good by vigorous psychology authentically displayed. Euripides' *Medea* has the familiar explanatory domestics, but the heroine herself is vibrantly alive, most cogently real. The bad method may be watched almost any day, and Shakespeare himself supplies a capital example in *Julius Cæsar*. The dictator is a mere simulacrum to which an external glow of life is imparted only by the comments of others,

> Why, man, he doth bestride the narrow world
> Like a Colossus,

and the rest.

Between this method and the third, "the attitude of persons who have been in close touch with him," there may seem little difference or none. What is exactly meant, however, is not their verbal attitude towards him only, but their outlook on things, their own minor psychology, shown by their reaction to his influence. If we compare *Julius Cæsar* with Ibsen's *Master Builder*, we see at once how much more powerfully and intimately the Norwegian has created his main character by means of Solness' wife and employees, than the Englishman has succeeded in projecting a real figure even by the eloquence of Cassius or of Antony. Shakespeare does, however, at other times wield this instrument superbly; witness the perfectly dramatic and illuminating manner in which Enobarbus reacts to Cleopatra, Cassio and Emilia to Iago. Indeed, though this device is a favourite of Ibsen's, who uses it again and again with miraculous power (as in *The Wild Duck* and *Hedda*

Gabler), the example from *Othello* is perhaps the strongest and most arresting proof of its possibilities. Iago himself is a puzzle: his character of unredeemed evil is a psychological problem that has baffled the greatest. What we realize of him is learnt from the attitude of others; we cannot look him in the face, but must scan his lineaments, as did Perseus those of the Gorgon, in a mirror.

There remain the first two means of characterization—the things done, the words said, by the person himself. These two are different but inseparable; together they constitute the most difficult, most interesting, most valuable, and (next to plot itself) most necessary task of the dramatist. In the first place, it is clear that the playwright must imagine his character definitely and then present him performing appropriate deeds, uttering appropriate words. So far, the work is not specially difficult. Most people can imagine a brave, patriotic, military officer who should (owing to " machinations ") fall under a cloud and be publicly degraded. They can also cause him at the critical moment to strike an attitude and cry : " You may take away my sword, but you cannot take away my Victoria Cross ! "

If this is all that one needs, why is *One of the Best* less admirable than *Henry the Fifth*? We need much more. So far we have only cut out a figure in the flat, and this is not creation at all. The genuine dramatic master makes characters in three dimensions; we can walk all round them, envisage them from unobvious angles, feel that we know them, not merely see them. They stand on their own feet, detached from the background which happens to be placed behind them at the moment, ready to walk into other environments, encountering fresh companions and new enterprises. That is the one test of a great character study; we instinctively imagine them in surroundings not depicted by the author—" Micawber would have done so-and-so! " " What would Sir Willoughby Patterne have said ? " A celebrated example relates to the best-drawn figure in all literature: *The Merry Wives of Windsor* was written because of Elizabeth's curiosity to see Falstaff in love.

But how is this done ? By what devices does an author make his people " come alive " ? Here, of course, we approach a region where there seems to be no footing—the attempt to explain how genius brings itself to bear. It is, nevertheless, worth while to make the attempt, though an adequate account is naturally out of the question. Sometimes a character grows on the author's hands without his conscious volition. He imagines a person of minor calibre, restricted importance; then it happens that the man or woman so imagined appeals to the writer's own temperament—"grows on him"—and becomes too great for his environment. So it was, we know, that Samuel Pickwick developed; so, in all likelihood, Shylock grew from a sordid scoundrel to the colossal representative of a whole nation, an immemorial history clothed in a single yellow gaberdine. But normally, no doubt, such vivid creations are evolved with full consciousness. How? The dramatist ponders his proposed character not at first in the environment which is to be his upon the stage. He lives in his company, sits down to meat with him, walks in his society through street, market, and meadow; watches his love-making and quarrels, reads the same book over his shoulder; discusses with him religion, war, politics, commerce; shares his jests and reads the meditation of his heart. All this is at first only the terrific travail and joy of creation, but little by little the strain of conscious toil becomes the delighted watching of a creature which hourly takes to itself as by miracle a seemingly independent life, though never, as in our earlier instances, too great for its surroundings. Hans Andersen, when he wrote the fantasy of the man who lost his shadow, was composing an allegory of all great fiction. Then, when the imagined man or woman is complete, then, and not till then, is the name Falstaff or Portia given, and the Eastcheap tavern roars with vital gusto shed abroad by a being more human than any man in the theatre, the terraces of Belmont are flooded with the sunny radiance of one who sums up in her sweet presence the charm and strength of many women. Of the hundred conversations which Shakespeare held with Cleopatra, of all those valiant affrays wherein he charged stirrup by stirrup with Talbot or Hotspur, of those many conferences in camp and court with Roman triumvirs, Plantagenet kings, and Tudor nobles, but little has escaped on to paper. The poet knew Falstaff in his slender youth, Lady Macbeth as a girl at her sampler and her prayers, Mark Antony in doublet and trunk-hose taking boat for Hampton Court, Prospero as a neighbour gossiping of crops and herds by a Stratford fireside, Rosalind nursing her babies or seeking her lost husband upon some nameless battlefield. It is because the life which these superb men and women passed in his peerless imagination was vaster far than the few events which unroll themselves before our eyes in the Arden Forest, on the banks of old Nile, or along the corridors of Dunsinane, that when we meet them in these surroundings we salute them as more real than ourselves.

All this might be put crudely by a mere reminder that such persons make other remarks, and do other things, than are in strictness called for by their situation; there is a *largior æther* about their talk and conduct. One main reason for the impression of triviality left by many plays is that the persons keep closely and unsuggestively to the matter in hand. Whenever Harpagon appears we know that he will talk about money. But, on the other side, we shall not make a character vivid by the mere bestowal of irrelevant conversation; it will not do to hang upon his part sundry tags of extraneous chat "to give atmosphere."

His author must conceive him from the centre outwards. The actual written evidence of such complete imagination as we have tried to expound will of course vary from character to character. Among Shakespeare's greatest figures Macbeth perhaps shows this evidence least. Needless to say, he is none the less magnificent for that; but his darkly terrific speeches are based on a comparatively narrow *expressed* reminiscence of the thousand daily concerns and activities shared by average men. Hamlet certainly shows such evidence most, going beyond the network of microscopic allusion which we have most in mind to definite, sometimes elaborate, disquisition, as in his memories of Yorick and (still more) in his interview with the strolling players.

The mention of Hamlet tempts us into a digression. One of our most brilliant and esteemed dramatic critics, Mr. A. B. Walkley, in an essay [1] entitled "Professor Bradley's *Hamlet*," has set forth a view diametrically opposite to that suggested in the two preceding paragraphs. We may well draw encouragement to embrace our own theory from the extraordinary vagaries into which

[1] *Drama and Life*, pp. 148–55.

Mr. Walkley is plunged by fidelity to his own. For example, he asserts that such comments as " Doubtless in happier days he [Hamlet] was a close and constant observer of men and manners " show Professor Bradley " unconsciously wandering into speculations about Hamlet as a real person, existing off the stage, and independently of Shakespeare's play." And whither is the critic led by his hostility to this method ? To nothing less than this: that Shakespeare did not care whether his characters were credible or not, that he is just as pleased to fling a heap of odds and ends on to the stage with the remark, " These are Hamlet," as to create a credible being ! It may appear impossible that any man who has read the poet for ten minutes should offer such statements, but here are Mr. Walkley's words : "Shakespeare himself had these characteristics, and sought expression for them on the stage without a perpetual solicitude for consistency or intelligibility in his mouthpiece. A father is addressing his son starting on a journey. Shakespeare sees the ' good things ' appropriate to that situation in general, and at once puts them in the mouth of Polonius, though it suits him afterwards to make Polonius a 'tedious old fool.' . . . The theme of the moment was 'A Father's Advice to his Son' or 'The Art of Acting' or 'Meditations on Suicide,' and all the dramatic resources of that theme were duly 'exploited' on the spot." In a passage like this we may watch the art of dramatic criticism committing suicide.

Returning now to the main theme of which characterization is one department,—"that which the persons do themselves,"—we have to treat of their work in carrying out the plot. The reader may object that characters are only created and revealed precisely by such motion and execution. Certainly; but for clearness' sake it is necessary to sunder in discussion things actually combined, just as the anatomist studies a single organ which does not, however, function by itself. We proceed then to action, the things done and said by our characters. By their influence upon one another, their mutual reactions, they give body to the plot. Plot is the "soul of the play," as Aristotle put it, action is its flesh, the characters are its organs. Dramatic manner consists in the confrontation of people whose purposes, interests, powers, have a clear relationship of cause and effect, of tendency and obstacle, of aim and opposing aim. It is this condition of intense contrast between persons standing in one another's presence which is most usually implied by the word " dramatic." [1] In the two highest types of drama, tragedy and comedy, this confrontation is of a special and most momentous kind—the collision of personalities which are the vehicle of opposing ideas, whereas in the other types the collision is between people who stand for nothing more than their own concerns.

The author of tragedy or of comedy, owing allegiance both to the abstract governing idea and to the particular human being who is its vehicle, must be true to both. But how ? If the person is to express the idea adequately, what room is there for the individual marks needed to make him " real " ? If, on the other side, he is to be

[1] Mr. William Archer, in his chapter "Dramatic and Undramatic" (*Playmaking*, pp. 23-41), repudiates the doctrine that drama is the presentment of struggle, and suggests (p. 29) that "the essence of drama is *crisis.*" These statements, as general statements, are excellent. It will be seen that the present writer insists on "collision" only in the highest types of drama, and later in this essay the importance of crisis is developed at length. But a general condition of contrast between the persons is always an ingredient in dramatic method.

a convincingly human creature, will not the universality of the idea evaporate? Here is the deepest problem of great drama; and it is perhaps the most splendid artistic triumph of the human spirit that it has achieved a number of amazingly good solutions. Æschylus is the supreme instance of a mind filled with the profoundest abstract truths yet expressing them within the limits of particular time, place, and personality; his theological concept of imperfect godhead rising to omniscience, omnipotence, universal benevolence, is magnificently conveyed through Orestes, Prometheus, and others without spoiling the individual clearness of the persons. His people are, to be sure, drawn with simple, sweeping lines; there is none of that fine brushwork which a modern master of anything like Æschylus' calibre would give, and which Euripides—even Sophocles, in some degree—has given. But he has endowed them with as much personal colour as was possible without blurring the eternal facts whose messengers and offspring they are. He has held the scales marvellously level, for his profound sense of God and his vivid sense of Man were equally powerful.

Without that balance we might have found in his pages a jejune presentation of abstractions like the featureless Virtues and Vices of a morality-play. Something like this, indeed, happened when Shelley imitated his *Prometheus*: the English poet gives us no characters, only qualities endowed with vocal chords.

No other dramatist has kept universal and particular so evenly matched. Ibsen, perhaps, comes nearest to Æschylus in this respect. Hedda Gabler is artistically the modern Prometheus. Yet even she is more "interesting," as we call it—that is, we are more concerned with her individual surroundings than with those of Prometheus. Goethe's *Faust*, again, gives often more weight to the ideal than to the particular. The earlier scenes are gloriously Æschylean, but as the drama progresses the universal more and more clearly overrides the specific and individual, until at the close we hear the "chorus mysticus" singing pure Platonism:—

>Alles Vergängliche
>Ist nur ein Gleichniss;
>Das Unzulängliche
>Hier wird's Ereigniss;
>Das Unbeschreibliche
>Hier ist es gethan;
>Das Ewig-weibliche
>Zieht uns hinan.

This is magnificent, but it is not drama. It is too deep, too ultimate; and a playwright's business is not to expound the ultimate directly (even supposing he can), but to translate it into terms of credibly particular men, women, and human action. All other modern dramatists, except Shakespeare in his greatest work, will be found stressing either the super-human (or indeed infra-human) idea or the particular example in hand. The latter method has in modern times been far more common and successful. In this region Euripides alone of Greek dramatists can be compared with Shakespeare and Ibsen; no figure drawn by Æschylus, Sophocles, or Aristophanes, can rival in vividness his Phædra, his Medea, his Orestes.

The struggle between the idea conveyed and the character-vehicle has not only tended to depress one or the other: it has influenced character-drawing itself, especially in comedy. Hence arises the drama of types instead of strongly individualized persons, the most notable kind being the comedy of manners. Molière is its greatest exponent; his lovers, rogues, simpletons, are little more than the greatest common measure of all the members of each class. Such a method strikes one on *a priori* grounds as unpromising, and in fact Molière's vast charm and power are found far less in psychology than in dialogue. Ben Jonson belongs to the same school; his reputation (such as it is, for he is but *magni nominis umbra*) depends not on characterization but on a brisk jumble of action. His *Bartholomew Fair* provides perhaps the best specimen in dramatic literature of that famous desideratum, the " slice of life." But the " humours " which he so industriously exhibits give little entertainment; when they are unsupported by other attractions the result is dreariness unspeakable: *Every Man out of his Humour* is possibly the most unreadable work ever penned. Congreve, like Molière, is saved from such an abyss by brilliant dialogue. Tragedy, as we said, has suffered less than comedy from this attempt to achieve universality by cutting away peculiarities—a sure way to produce what is less, not more, human than our next-door neighbour. But it may be observed even at the highest levels; Sophocles shows at times, especially in *Antigone*, a hardness of surface which is due to this cause.

Our personages, then, whether they convey such fundamental ideas as a new conception of Providence or whether they are merely endeavouring to anticipate one another in the search for stolen bonds, meet before our eyes in personal impact. Between the main characters or groups of characters there is collision, not necessarily hostile collision, but a confrontation of unlike aims, opinions, or instincts. Between Macbeth and his wife, between Alceste and Célimène in *Le Misanthrope*, between Tanner and Ann Whitefield in *Man and Superman*, between Bluntschli and Raina in *Arms and the Man*, there is no hostility, but such an impact of dissimilar temperaments that by the resulting heat the plot is moulded. It is, of course, even more obvious that consciously hostile collision provides the very core of countless plays: it is enough to quote, for conscious hostility on both sides, *Prometheus Vinctus, Antigone, Coriolanus, The Merchant of Venice*; and, for consciousness on one side only, the *Choephoræ, Medea, Othello*. While the chief persons thus come into marked collision, there is frequently between two minor characters some kind of clash, however minute. It varies from the fatal

OF DRAMA

duel of Tybalt and Mercutio, through the contrast between Kent and the Fool during their attendance upon Lear, to the jars between Sebastian and Gonzalo in *The Tempest*, or the distinctions in rascality exhibited by Pistol and Nym. Even lords-in-waiting and nameless bystanders are divided by plain variations of sympathy or opinion.

It will be remembered that our present topic is action, not plot; we are not yet concerned with the development of the question-and-answer construction, but only with the commerce between the persons from moment to moment. Under this head one topic remains—intensity. The action must be neat and crisp; things should happen with what may be described as a click. The mere entry of some one with a seeming-casual remark may in the circumstances have the effect of an explosion. At the end of the Third Act of Hervieu's *La Course du Flambeau* occurs this minute " scene " :—

MME. FONTENAIS (*revenant de sa chambre*) : Eh bien ? . . . Où en es-tu, entre ta mère et ta fille ? Suis-je du voyage ?

SABINE (*répondant d'un signe de tête plutôt que de la voix*) : Oui.

In another place this would be nothing. Set where it is, it is intensely dramatic. Not only does it doom the mother to death; it is the core of the plot and voices the moral of the whole piece. Few plays equal *La Course du Flambeau* in this special quality, but all playwrights more or less clearly realize the need. So strongly, in fact, do writers of our time feel the importance of crisp action that they have evolved what is called the "curtain"—that is, the device of closing an act or scene at the highest possible point of tension. An excellent example has just been given from Hervieu; but many others may be found with ease. So in *Mrs. Gorringe's Necklace*, by Mr. H. H. Davies, the First Act ends just after we have discovered that David Cairn is the thief and exactly at the moment when his *fiancée* innocently induces him to agree, with a breaking heart, that everything shall be "like the old times." But a morbid passion for the "strong curtain" has led some writers of farce and melodrama to strange lengths. They bring it about not artistically but mechanically, as a rule by the sudden reappearance of some interesting person whom the audience has half-forgotten and who is now unexpectedly and irrationally thrust forward into a scene already tense. *Are you a Mason?* contains a crude instance of this. Much less objectionable, but similar, is the laughable moment in M. Rostand's *Chantecler* when at the end of the long and tumultuous reception held by the Guinea-Hen, the curtain descends just as the usher announces "The Tortoise!" Like this, but entirely, indeed splendidly, justified is the craftsmanship whereby Augier, in his *La Pierre de Touche*, after mentioning a character several times, but never presenting him, at length causes him to be announced, and ends the whole play with the words "Faites entrer." It is a masterly stroke, because though this lieutenant's future influence upon the hero's fortunes is important and necessary to complete the plot, we need nothing more than this crisp reminder of the form which that influence is certain to take.

One delightful and frequent method of securing the "click" is to employ "business" with material objects or exciting features of real life. This method, again, is often childishly dragged into the lower dramatic types, as in the racecourse scenes and criminal trials of melodrama. But there are a thousand examples of its admirable employment — the meeting of employers and strikers in Mr. Galsworthy's *Strife*, the mannequin scene in *The Madras House* of Mr. Barker, the rehearsal in Meilhac-Halévy's *Froufrou*; and the brilliant use of material objects may be observed in countless plays, from the purple carpets in the *Agamemnon* and the bow of Philoctetes to Portia's caskets, Desdemona's handkerchief, and the floating crutch of the drowned Eyolf.

Two portions of "that which the persons do themselves" have now been indicated— characterization and action. The third, dialogue or speech, remains. In few respects do dramatic authors differ more widely. Sometimes it is not genuine dialogue at all, but a succession of tirades; others employ nothing but short sentences, ostensibly the exact replica of everyday talk; and various stages between these extremes are to be noted. Nor is length the only standard of difference. Poetic form or poetic diction or both are employed by some; others write prose; a third class write neither— for M. Jourdain was absurdly wrong—but keep to the formless speech of ordinary folk; a fourth kind, finally, compose a queer stilted jargon which can best be described as sanctified journalese. Each length-difference can of course be combined with any of the style-differences. Thus, to take but a few examples, we find in Sophocles poetic form, poetic diction, and long speeches; poetic form, poetic diction, and short speeches in Rostand; prosaic form, poetic diction, and short speeches in Maeterlinck; prosaic form, prosaic diction, and long speeches in Shaw.

Ignoring details, we find that the great difference lies in the choice between poetical and prose form. The tendency to poetry has been caused in great degree by the influence of other literature; in Greece, for example, by the prestige of epic and by the lyrics which formed an integral part of Greek drama. Another cause is the desire to distinguish emphatically the language of an art-form from that of every day. The use of prose, and of short sentences, is due to the search for verisimilitude, but this has been modified by the influence just mentioned in connexion with poetry—the desire for artistic diction; the finest result in our time of these two tendencies is the work of J. M. Synge.

Each form has its peculiar danger. In poetic drama it is irrelevance, the playwright being constantly tempted to develop a theme altogether beyond what its dramatic value demands, for the sake of its own poetical possibilities.[1] Undoubtedly a beautiful long speech may be thoroughly dramatic : every lovely phrase or pungent stroke of rhetoric may serve the plot or aid characterization. Antony's funeral oration is a superb proof of this. Prospero's narrative to Miranda at the opening of *The Tempest* and (far more) the soliloquies of Macbeth are all dramatic timber as well as poetry excellent or sublime in itself. But the Queen Mab speech of Mercutio and the equally exquisite description of the bees' commonwealth in *Henry the Fifth* are on an altogether different plane ; they are intruded into the action, which they only delay and serve not at all. Mercutio's speech, it may be objected, illustrates his character. But it is illustrated enough

---

[1] Mr. C. E. Montague (*Dramatic Values*, p. 227) roundly says of the *Récits de Théramène* : " They are magnificent, but not drama." As a matter of fact the original " narrative of Theramenes," in Racine's *Phèdre* (V. vi.), is perfectly dramatic (and exactly in the tradition of the Messengers' Speeches in Greek tragedy).

otherwise; the purpose is answered at least equally well by such things as: " 'Tis not so deep as a well, nor so wide as a church-door; but 'tis enough . . . ask for me to-morrow, and you shall find me a grave man." It is, indeed, plain that *Romeo and Juliet* as a whole provides a gloriously beautiful specimen of transition-form; it is lyric passing into drama, much as Peele's *Old Wives' Tale* is narrative passing into drama. No one doubts that such disquisitions are brought in only to gratify the sense of literary beauty, and with no thought of the plot.[1] It is of no avail to point out that poets who compose for theatres with a platform, so to call it—the Greek theatre, if the actors played in the orchestra, and the Elizabethan theatre with its "apron"— naturally find themselves writing elaborate recitations which the performer declaims to his audience like an orator on the tribune. This (even if true) does nothing more than account for the poet's own standard of length in speeches: it has no bearing on their

---

[1] There is no recantation here of what was said concerning Mr. A. B. Walkley's remarks on Hamlet. We only remark that such passages do not help the drama as drama; Mr. Walkley believes without misgiving that they may stultify it.

relevance. All we can say is that the conditions render the temptation to irrelevance greater for Euripides and Shakespeare than for Ibsen, Hauptmann, and Hervieu. Rhetoric, moralizing, preaching may be perfectly dramatic, however long. We objected just now on technical grounds to Mercutio's Queen Mab " effort." But take another passage from the same play. Friar Laurence muses upon his simples :—

> The grey-ey'd morn smiles on the frowning night,
> Checkering the eastern clouds with streaks of light,

and so forth for thirty lines in all. It is a memorable speech, but apparently quite static. Then what, we ask, has this quiet musing to do with the fortunes of the young lovers? Is it any more to the purpose than the fantasia of Mercutio? It is, in fact, vastly more dramatic. First, it plainly conveys an allegory of Romeo's waywardness and of the wasteful enmity between Montagues and Capulets. Secondly, it is in tune with the situation. The Friar is alone, at complete leisure, an aged man taking the morning air outside his cell. Moralizing for its own sake is here far more natural than that a young gallant, amid companions agog for a frolic, should detain them with highly-wrought *fioriture*, however exquisite, on the topic of dreams, while they postpone their business to listen attentively in a semicircle, as no party of young men ever did since the world began.

The main danger of prose-dialogue is more insidious. We saw that prose is employed in order to give verisimilitude, but that the artist's instinct recoils from complete likeness; art makes a picture, not a photograph. Thus the prose-dramatist is threatened on the one side by commonness, on the other by unreality. He must somehow portray, at times, the banal or stupid without losing all dignity and vivacity; but if he writes so that every one exclaims " How unnatural! " he has failed. The whole topic of " truth to life " cannot well be treated here, though it plainly affects dialogue no less than character, action, and plot. Still it may be said that it is infinitely better to imitate real talk exactly than to recoil from it into the jargon which now reads so incredibly in the English drama of seventy years ago. In the second act of Mr. Shaw's *Major Barbara* occur passages which render with complete realism the conversation and conduct of the slums; in *Pygmalion* he brought upon the stage a word hitherto supposed securely unprintable. Objection has been taken to such fidelity. But compare it with the other extreme, quoted [1] by Mr. Walkley from a play highly popular in its time (1841), Boucicault's *London Assurance*:

> I love to watch the first tear that glistens in the opening eye of morning, the silent song that flowers breathe, the thrilling choir of the woodland minstrels, to which the modest brook trickles applause; these, swelling out the sweetest chord of sweet creation's matins, seem to pour some soft and merry tale into the daylight's ear, as if the waking world had dreamed a happy thing, and now smiled o'er the telling of it.

The rule for prose-dialogue is plain. It must be like enough to actual speech for us to imagine ourselves joining in it tomorrow morning, but more forceful, neater, richer, and—unless characterization demands this—unencumbered by the half-articulated scraps of phrase which spread fungus-like over the conversation of most people. This rule, like so many others, is of small use without experience, and a commencing playwright who has been alarmed by Boucicault

[1] *Drama and Life*, pp. 14 et seq.

and his peers will produce by reaction dialogue which is bald and stringy. Seeking a remedy for this, he will take to crude cleverness: people who are not witty *ex hypothesi* will nevertheless talk wittily; others will unconsciously reveal their failings by a neat maladroitness for which we sigh vainly in the real world; others will interrupt one another and create a joke by accidental collaboration. Such devices in moderation are well enough, but they do not by themselves constitute excellent dialogue. Wit is, indeed, the regular stopping-place of good second-rate dramatists; only the master goes beyond it. The manner of Oscar Wilde is here most instructive. His dialogue falls into two sharply sundered divisions: the serious, when it is pretentious, hysterical, or dull; and the witty, when it is mostly irrelevant, though blazing with unmatchable epigrams. It is never what it should be, thoroughly good normal conversation. A lady suddenly remarks, " Define women for me." Pat comes the response: " Sphinxes without secrets." Such things are very delightful, but they should be published in the form of La Rochefoucauld's *Maximes et Réflexions Morales*; they do not justify the substructure of Adams drawing-rooms, French windows, secret cheque-books, and the like. In this sphere the unchallenged master is Ibsen. His conversations are always vibrant, whatever the topic, but never florid and never bald—unless, as we said, the character-study definitely requires such qualities. Every word is interesting, but he is never merely witty; as some are too happy to need amusement, so is he too brilliant to need wit. His conversations glow continuously instead of flashing and crackling at intervals. All this is apart from their greatest virtue, that of assisting the plot with an effortless mastery which is perhaps Ibsen's most splendid merit.

The three divisions of our subject have now been in some measure described: the nature, the aim, and the methods of drama. But it is imperative that we should examine more closely the nature of plot, the Formal Cause (as Aristotle might have said) of the action—the shape which makes it what it is. How must action be modelled or kneaded if it is to be dramatic? The main rule, we saw, was that it should first definitely pose a question, some riddle to be solved, or some tangle to be unravelled, and that it should as definitely offer the reply, the solution, the unravelling—what in French is called the *dénouement,* or "untying." We must now go further. The next consideration is economy—to draw from every datum in the situation, every character, every scene, every speech, the utmost assistance for the purpose of the whole, and to employ the minimum number of factors. This is by no means the same thing as simplicity. An admirably economical play will often be found complex in its delicate adjustment and reaction of parts, *e.g. Œdipus Tyrannus* and *Hedda Gabler*; whereas many plays of rudimentary structure contain a lavish apparatus of minor persons or scenic changes, *e.g. Peter Pan, Chantecler,* and *Peer Gynt.* Let us now indicate some important results of the instinct for economy.

First, the solution should be given entirely in terms of the original question. We said above that it must "come out" of the question, in order to include even the worst dramas, where the main characters settle their difficulty, or (more often) find it settled for them, by the aid of novel factors violently intruded at, or later than, the middle of the play. Instead of working out a problem based (let us say) on their poverty, by using their own abilities, their own surroundings, and the experience or opportunities which their poverty itself can and must supply, they observe near the close of the last act but one a quaint whiteheaded figure approach their house, scanning the numbers. In a few minutes they learn that it is their Uncle Peter from New South Wales, whose existence has been hitherto concealed both from them and from the audience; he has amassed a gigantic fortune from sheep-farming, he has not married, and has come home to die. Despite the concern with which they listen to his hacking cough, they cannot but see that their financial troubles are nearing the end. Such a solution " comes out " of the situation as originally set; the people, the local conditions, and the rest, are mostly unchanged. But there is no necessary tie between end and beginning; the structure is wretchedly bad. Uncle Peter is in fact the ancient *deus ex machina*, heavily secularized for the delectation of an age which has rejected religious myth but still cherishes myths of finance. The " god from the machine " is a thoroughly bad device, simply because he cuts the knot instead of untying it. The knot is there to be untied; it is skill in doing so which is a leading proof of good craftsmanship, and which affords the spectator his strongest thrill of interest. Analogous powers or events elsewhere in the drama are not necessarily bad. Thus the whole action of *Hamlet* is launched by a supernatural visitation. The Prince could not learn the facts in any other way; and, granted a public which effectually believes in ghosts, such an opening is perfectly sound. It is far otherwise when the action of *A Winter's Tale* is turned upside down by the intrusion of an unusually clear and complete response from the Delphic Oracle. But the magical elements in *The Tempest* and *A Midsummer Night's Dream* are quite unobjectionable; superhuman powers are constantly and from the first postulated for Prospero and Oberon. Objection lies against the sudden introduction of miraculous shortcuts into purely human situations. What should we say if Puck strayed into *The Merchant of Venice* and converted "The Duke, Magnificoes, and train" to Judaism? In brief, the ideal plot provides an answer which in its entirety is latent in the problem.

The persons, acting upon one another by their psychology, by discoveries about one another's aims or opinions made through sudden confrontation, by the persuasions and enlightenments of dialogue, manipulate the difficulty which enmeshes them all in their several degrees, until it exhibits a new design made from its original elements. Sympathy is born, resignation, comfort, understanding. "Latent in the problem," we said. The materials for a solution should all be present, but it is plainly wrong to leave things so obvious that any spectator can prophesy the end. The entertainment provided by good drama is a curious blend of the sense of probability and the sense of surprise. Probability must never harden into inevitability, nor surprise into disbelief. The action swings over upon itself, the end keeps tryst with the beginning—"The wheel is come full circle, I am here." This close interweaving of fabric is a leading difference between drama and other literary forms.

A second feature of economy is to be observed in the management of character. First, each person's psychology must subserve the plot. Those qualities in Lear which the First Act reveals—his love for his daughters, his imperiousness, whimsicality, and childish temper, form not only a marvellous study in themselves, but a power influencing the action at every turn. Macbeth's valour is shown by the sergeant's story; his superstition by the disturbance awakened in him by the witches' greeting; his ambition by the deep effect on his mind which their promise exercises. None of these qualities would have availed without the others to bring about his crimes; Duncan's murder, the usurpation, Banquo's death, the butchery in Fife, all are caused by this trinity, valour, superstition, ambition. That Othello is unused to polite Venetian society seems at first a thing of no moment; we may even ask ourselves why Shakespeare has gone out of his way to substitute a negro for the apparently obvious Italian *condottiero*. But here lies what one is tempted to call the most masterly device that even Shakespeare ever conceived. This ignorance of Othello's proves to be the one means whereby Iago's devilish cunning can persuade him that Desdemona is unfaithful. Had Judge Brack shown himself in the least degree less self-complacent in his dealings with Hedda

Gabler, probably she would not have killed herself after all; his sleek security is the finishing touch. Euripides' Hippolytus on his first appearance delivers an exquisitely beautiful address to his patroness-deity Artemis. So lovely is it that we perhaps do not observe the evidence it affords of an excessive relish for subtle emotion: the evidence has to be underlined by his brief colloquy with the aged serving-man. But it is this relish which later betrays Hippolytus into a refined gloating over Phædra's distress and persuades the over-tried woman to destroy him. A second economy in the management of character is to lay upon each person more than one function. The chief figures are naturally so employed; but the able playwright will be found providing a double duty for minor characters too: they support and are supported like the stones of an arch. This admirable contrivance aids in a high degree the desired tautness, the sense of grip. Bassanio serves to bring Shylock and Antonio into collision by his necessities; then through his marriage with Portia he occasions Antonio's rescue. In *Henry the Fourth* Prince Hal forms the link between Falstaff's group and the public issues treated by the play. Louka in Mr. Shaw's *Arms and the Man* performs the quite separate functions of a foil to Raina in Saranoff's eyes, and of a means to bring Raina and Bluntschli together. If we turn to ancient drama we find that this method lies at the very root of Terence's magnificent dramaturgy: he loves to pose a double question and solve the two parts by their very interdependence. Euripides' *Hecuba* contains a most curious example: an aged slave, who is sent to fetch water for Polyxena's burial-rites, discovers Polydorus' corpse while so busied, and thus actually makes the only bond between the two portions of the tragedy. A far more skilful instance is Io in the *Prometheus* of Æschylus. She draws from the hero some of his most interesting speeches; she exemplifies in her own person once more the cruelty of Zeus, whom Prometheus is defying; and she points forward to his rescuer Heracles, her own descendant. It is naturally not often that the absence of such double functioning is noticed as a distinct flaw; but in the *Francillon* of Dumas *fils* it is plainly a serious weakness that the heroine's supposed lover proves to be a man who has no other real concern with the plot; he ought to have been one of the family-friends to whom we are introduced at the outset. It need scarcely be said that many minor characters perform one duty only without æsthetic offence, and have important relations with not more than one person—the physicians and clowns, the lords and citizens, Audrey, Tubal, Charmian, and a hundred more, the " feeders," confidants, and purveyors of information. Even in far simpler casts than Shakespeare's they are to be found—the watchman in *Antigone* and the numerous heralds from Æschylus' *Supplices* downwards. Euripides' tendency is to take over such characters and mortise them into the plot: a comparison of Pylades in the *Choephoræ* of Æschylus with Pylades in the Euripidean *Orestes* is most instructive.

The third great use of economy is in dialogue. Here as elsewhere an important distinction holds between romantic and classic drama. In the ideal classic play there would not be a single word which gave no help to the development of the plot; in the ideal romantic play, dialogue would be often expanded, not perhaps for the sake merely of a " purple patch " (the question which we discussed above), but to impress upon us more vividly the momentary situation (*e.g.* the poverty of Romeo's Mantuan apothecary), and so less directly than in the classical type to further the action. So much is true in theory, but there is no ideal instance of either form. Sophocles, on the whole the most " classical " of all playwrights, does develop speeches, if not conversations, for the sake of " romantic " momentary vividness, as Œdipus shows in the *Coloneus* and Teucer in *Ajax*, since (to be pedantic) the defence of Œdipus and the praises of Ajax could have been put effectively in fewer words. On the other side, many passages in which Shakespeare might seem to delay the plot for the sake of " getting in " a structurally useless speech will be found to perform a genuinely dramatic function. Juliet's Nurse insists on relating a brisk anecdote of her late husband. What connexion can it claim with the plot ? This : the remarkable fact needs explanation, that the Nurse makes no difficulty whatever in aiding her extremely young mistress to carry on a love affair and contract a marriage without the knowledge of her parents. To understand this we must see her as what she is, a nerveless invertebrate mass of hypertrophied sentiment. Nothing could show this better than the talk assigned to her, whereas a third-rate poet would have left her uncharacterized, settling all scruples about responsibility with the words " Here's gold for thee ! " The two methods in dialogue do, then, often merge into one another ; but the difference in tendency is unmistakable. Ibsen is in this department even more " classical," in his realist dramas, than Sophocles. If we take a sentence at random from *An Enemy of the People,* our finger lights upon Stockmann's question to the Burgomaster : " Can you suggest any other plan ? " These words extract from the Burgomaster an expression of opinion about Stockmann's report on the town water-supply, and so directly bring Stockmann into collision with the community. So it is everywhere in this dramatist's most significant work. Herein lies one reason for the quality of his influence. His dialogue is close-grained and absorbing, hardly ever airy, *dégagé*. Even at its sprightliest it conveys a sense of creeping momentousness. Hence Ibsen is not " popular " : he is too solid, too concentrated for a genuine vogue with the multitude. But his thoughts are so profound and permanently applicable, his technical skill so stupendous, that his influence steadily filters down through dramatists, social theorists, students of literary art, experts in the theatre, to the innumerable average people who would not think of actually going to witness an Ibsen performance. Thus he has in England collaborated unseen not only with Mr. Shaw, Mr. Barker, and others of the new school, but also with playwrights who ostentatiously ignore him, such as Sir Arthur Pinero and Mr. H. A. Jones.

Returning to the main thread of this essay, we remind ourselves that two essential features of plot have now been discussed: the existence of an answered question, and the observance of economy. We now approach the third vital characteristic, the most important and attractive topic in the whole study of dramatic technique.

That topic has been partly anticipated by the statement that the solution should grow out of the problem. But there we were considering the nature of a good solution. We are now to discuss the principles of growth, the manner in which the relationship between answer and problem is made out; in short, how a plot is "worked." The first rule here is that laid down by Aristotle: that a drama must have a beginning, a middle, and an end. This looks absurdly obvious; but when the philosopher explains that by "beginning" is meant something naturally followed by something else, but not necessarily preceded by anything, that by "middle" is meant something which implies precedent and posterior events, and that an "end" is something naturally preceded, but not necessarily followed, by something else, we find at once in these dry phrases a useful standard of common sense in structure, and an explanation of the vague irritation caused in us by many so-called plays. Shaw's *Getting Married* has no middle and no end. Schnitzler's *Anatol* and Barrie's *Mary Rose* have no beginning, middle, or end; they start, go on, and leave off. Much has been already said of the first and last stages; we are now concerned mostly with "the middle."

Between the problem and the solution there must intervene a phase of the action which provides the material for the solution. From the whole of our preceding discussion, which showed collision, intensity, crispness, as qualities of drama, we should expect that our second stage, the portion which reveals the way to *dénouement*, would provide the required illumination not tamely or obviously, but through some kind of shock. Moreover, it is precisely here that the tautness and excitement reach their height; here is found the play's culmination. This phase of the action is named "crisis," "catastrophe," or (by Aristotle) "peripeteia." All these words mean more or less definitely the same thing. "Crisis" means literally "the act of judging," and in Greek medical science was applied to the point at which a disease took a turn for better or worse—"the critical moment." "Catastrophe" means "overthrow." "Peripeteia" is "falling over," "reversal," "recoil." All these etymologies indicate a fact which may be gathered inductively from innumerable plays; namely, that the peripeteia is not any and every increase of tension. The sudden return of Romeo and his slaying of Tybalt is not a peripeteia, nor is Macbeth's assassination of Duncan, nor Henry the Fifth's harangue on St. Crispin's Day, nor the scene where Faust watches the infernal hound "growing like an elephant" behind the stove in his study, nor Alceste's declamation of *Si le roi m'avait donné* in *Le Misanthrope*, nor the realization by Ramsden, in *Man and Superman*, that Tanner is his fellow-guardian, nor the first interview between Sabine and Stangy in *La Course du Flambeau*. All these, and hundreds more, are masterly, some of them sublime; their vigour, truth, and tenseness are beyond praise. But none of them is a peripeteia. The peripeteia is not only a culmination of some scene or situation : it is *the* culmination of the whole drama, providing (as we said) information or enlightenment necessary to the *dénouement*, and must show something more than vigour, truth, and intensity, though all these are demanded. That further quality is indicated by its names: there must be a "recoil," a sudden blow which alters the relations between person and person, between the various aspects of the situation. Let it be said at once that (although we may find bad catastrophes as easily as bad psychology or bad dialogue—"Uncle Peter," in fact) nothing here contradicts what has been said earlier about the use of accident or about organic connexion. The suddenness required is nothing more than an immense acceleration of normal development. The persons of the play have long been manipulating their difficulty until, like the glasses of a kaleidoscope, it falls over into a new pattern. Peripeteia is a readjustment, a complete change in the situation. As a general rule tragedy exhibits a peripeteia with three qualities: it is sudden, it is startling, it is illuminating. As a general rule, again, the peripeteia of comedy is simpler: one or two of these three qualities may be absent. Furthermore, some tragedies, like Æschylus' *Prometheus*, contain peripeteiæ analogous to those of comedy, and some comedies, such as Aristophanes' *Frogs*, at this point resemble tragedy. Perhaps the most exhilarating pursuit provided by literary criticism, and certainly the most indispensable part of dramatic criticism, is to examine each play that one reads or witnesses, asking, "Where precisely does the peripeteia occur?" and then to proceed with study of the whole structure. For it will occasionally be found that we have not after all clearly conceived "the question of the play," whether because we are misled by our own illogical interest in some minor point, or because the story is based upon real events familiar to us, and has yet been so remodelled that the leading interest of the drama differs somehow from the leading interest of the actual events.

In Sophocles' *Œdipus Tyrannus* the three great stages, Complication, Peripeteia, Solution, are unmistakable. The Complication is the necessity to find and expel from Thebes the man who slew Laius, since the pestilence will not cease before this is done. Œdipus, as king, takes measures to find the unknown murderer, until towards the end his ruthless questioning of the Herdsman reveals that the offender is himself, and that therefore he is not only the slayer looked for, but guilty of parricide and incest. That is the Catastrophe. Finally the *Dénouement* exhibits the Solution: the suicide of his mother Jocasta and his own self-blinding — acts which in some sort expiate his involuntary offences—and his determination to depart into exile. *Macbeth* is full of exciting and wonderful scenes, but the peripeteia is clearly the disillusionment of Macbeth when his magical defences fail. Here the "recoil" is double, or rather continued—Birnam Wood comes to Dunsinane, and later he is confronted by an adversary not "born of woman." But the suddenness is there; the catastrophe begins in a flash, marked (if we need a mark) by the King's sudden outcry, " Liar and slave ! " The difference is simply that the catastrophe itself lasts longer in *Macbeth* than in *Œdipus*. The reversal is equally plain in Shaw's *Major Barbara*: it is where Barbara Undershaft finds that the authorities of the Salvation Army are content to accept contributions from a distiller whose trade is one of the most powerful influences which they have to combat. This realization brings her world crashing about her ears; she at first feels that there is nothing left to live for. But this is only the peripeteia; as usual it is to provide a solution. Not only does this overthrow or recoil give the logical victory to her father's opposing point of view: far more than that, as soon as she grows calm she discovers that her real life-work, which she had supposed inextricable from her allegiance to the Salvation Army—the work, that is, of organizing social sanity and happiness—is not in fact dependent upon that allegiance, but can survive it; she goes on to perform the same task amid new surroundings. In *A Doll's House* the catastrophe occurs with the brief sentence of Torvald Helmer: "I don't want any melodramatic airs." All the rest of that famous scene is the *dénouement*, the working out of the solution which springs from the illumination brought to Nora by her husband's words. A beautiful catastrophe is found in Wilde's *Lady Windermere's Fan*. The play culminates in the brief passage where Mrs. Erlynne steps from behind the curtain, quietly claims the fan, and disappears. This leads to a brilliant *dénouement* wherein Lord Windermere and his wife have each relinquished their divergent views about Mrs. Erlynne and accepted one another's, and that because of the same fact.[1] Still more unmistakably, if possible, the peripeteia of *Mrs. Dane's Defence* occurs where the heroine confesses her identity with Felicia Hindemarsh; the whole play was written for the sake of its peripeteia. So probably was the *Venice Preserv'd* of Thomas Otway, a tragedy amazingly overrated; the only compensation for the falsetto blank verse, the emotional hysteria,

---

[1] How much credit Wilde himself deserves for this first-rate piece of construction is doubtful. See Mr. C. E. Montague, *Dramatic Values*, pp. 180 et seq.

and the babyish politics, is the discovery by Jaffier of Renault's design upon Belvidera, which discovery impels him finally to reveal the revolutionary plot and so produces a somewhat striking *dénouement* based upon Jaffier's agonized vacillation between love for Belvidera and love for Pierre.

Julius Cæsar is of the deepest interest in this connexion, as in so many others. Apparently, most readers assume that the catastrophe is the assassination of the dictator; but there are several objections to this view. First, does not the war between Brutus and Cassius, Antony and Octavius, become a curiously long and otiose addendum? Secondly (if we may begin to quote our own rules), where is the surprise which we noted as one of the three qualities shown by the tragic peripeteia? The murder of Julius has been clearly foreshadowed throughout the earlier scenes, and corresponds thus to the murder of Duncan. Moreover—though it must be confessed that this is an argument of doubtful relevance—this assassination was fatally familiar to Elizabethan audiences, as familiar as the result of Waterloo to a modern English audience. Fourthly, if this event is the culmination of the tragedy, why has the poet characterized Cæsar so feebly? This weakness has often been remarked; it seems strange that what might appear the finest moment in literature, the moment when the greatest of writers portrayed the greatest man of action, should be half-spoiled. Why has Shakespeare made Cæsar a far less engrossing figure than Hamlet, Othello, Macbeth, Shylock, and Falstaff? All these difficulties are solved if we merely content ourselves with looking at what the dramatist has done instead of what we assume he ought to have intended. If we look for a turn of events sudden, startling, and illuminating, we find it at once, not in the assassination, but in the thrilling emergence of Mark Antony as a formidable opponent of the republicans. The " question of the play " is not " What is to become of Cæsar ? " but " What is to become of the republican rising ? " Antony's Funeral Speech is the peripeteia, and the war which fills the later scenes is no addendum, but a magnificent and thoroughly appropriate *dénouement*.

It was remarked above that in comedy peripeteia tends to be less remarkable, or less distinguished as possessing all the three qualities we mentioned, than it is in tragedy. If we turn to Aristophanes, perhaps the world's greatest comic genius, this impression will be deepened. In the *Plutus*, the peripeteia or recoil is the recovery of sight by the blind god of wealth, which is followed by an effective solution or *dénouement*. But the catastrophe is not sudden; it is foretold and elaborately prepared. Nevertheless it is startling and illuminating. Here, and in most of this playwright's work the peripeteia arrives much earlier than elsewhere, and in most it is of the comparatively mild type. His peripeteia usually occurs at the consummation of the topsy-turvy idea with which the play opens—what Heine called the *Weltvernichtungsidee*. In *The Acharnians* the tension rises steadily until the preposterous private peace between a single Athenian citizen and the Spartan confederacy is completed and confirmed by the overthrow of Lamachus, the bombastic champion of militarism. This victory is the peripeteia, fairly sudden, quite startling, but not markedly illuminating: the illumination has been given progressively. Nevertheless, the position has been radically altered. Then follows a long *dénouement*, with a farcical, not comic, presentation of the blessings thus secured. *The Peace* is closely similar; so is *The Birds* and most other comedies from the same pen. In Molière's *Tartuffe* the catastrophe occurs at the moment when Orgon crawls from beneath the table in complete disillusionment as to Tartuffe's character :—

> Voilà, je vous l'avoue, un abominable homme !
> Je n'en puis revenir, et tout ceci m'assomme.

This is surely a fine "recoil" or peripeteia, but it is neither sudden nor startling, for we have long known that Tartuffe is making love to Elmire, and have watched the rather elaborate preparation made by her for the enlightenment of Orgon. And enlightened he certainly is; the "illumination" we spoke of is provided in full measure.

Nevertheless, it is obvious that many comedies have catastrophes no less complete than those of the greatest tragedies. Even Aristophanes has at least one good example. In *The Frogs*, Dionysus, who has descended into Hades with the purpose of fetching Euripides back to life as the greatest tragedian, suddenly announces that he will take Æschylus instead; this peripeteia is technically akin to those of tragedy. That exquisite artist, Terence, has created a beautiful catastrophe in *The Brothers* : it is not any revelation about the love affairs, but Demea's change of front, caused by his own reflections on the rival theories of education and social amenity held by his brother and himself. Similarly, in the *Phormio*, the bigamy of Chremes is revealed to much purpose by the resourceful sycophant. Sheridan's *School for Scandal* provides by means of the celebrated screen a perfect peripeteia. Synge's *Playboy of the Western World* (though its fame depends upon superb dialogue, compared with which the plot is of small interest) contains an excellent peripeteia in the sudden appearance of the " murdered " father.

It is, on the other side, equally obvious that tragedies not infrequently exhibit catastrophes such as we have shown to be often present in comedy. That of *Othello* is gradual, conviction being pressed upon the hero more and more effectually in several scenes ; but it ends in a convulsion startling and (as it seems to Othello) illuminating. That of Æschylus' *Persæ*—the appalling announcement to the Persians of the utter overthrow at Salamis—is not illuminating until reinforced by the admonitions and prophecies uttered by the ghost of Darius.

In short, every drama has a peripeteia, whether more elaborate or less. There is always a reversal of the situation, a climax of tension which alters fundamentally the original posture of affairs. If any alleged drama contains no such feature, it is not a play at all. This dictum will cease to appear wantonly pedantic when we reflect that such works (for instance, Mr. Shaw's *Getting Married*) are felt on all hands to be unsatisfactory, and that we are only assigning a precise reason for this dissatisfaction.

Before we leave this part of our theme, something must be said concerning the preparation for the peripeteia. In the greatest plays we saw that the illumination provided comes suddenly. But however startled we may be when it arrives, we shall certainly be puzzled or antagonized unless the way has been paved for it. The catastrophe must be "led up to," in such a way that we accept it as reasonable without, however, having foreseen it. This applies to the most consummate tragedies. In others, and more frequently in comedy, we have observed preparations so elaborate and obvious that, illuminating as the climax is, and sudden as it often is, it is in these plays not startling. But the method of preparation for a perfect peripeteia needs examination. Frequently it takes the form of a whole scene, inserted (so to put it) for this purpose only. In *The Merchant of Venice* occurs a brief interview between Antonio, when in chains, and Shylock. Short as it is, this passage is highly valuable to the plot. First, it brings home to us the realization of the Jew's purpose: it is the complement to the earlier interview in which the bargain was struck. Further, we obtain artistic pleasure from the reversal of positions: he who before was the fawning inferior stands forth as the arrogant master; he who lorded it with easy pride now begs indulgence. But—most important of all—we are quietly prepared for the approaching swing-round of sympathy. If we are to feel during the trial scene as the poet wishes us to feel, we must have rid ourselves of that irritation against Antonio, that sympathy with Shylock, which the early part of the drama has naturally awakened. Shakespeare has set this scene, at first sight so trifling, just in this place for just this purpose; he means to obliterate a great deal of the emotion aroused by that unanswerable outburst beginning

> Signior Antonio, many a time and oft,
> In the Rialto, you have rated me
> About my monies, and my usances.

Another, and far finer, example is afforded by *Macbeth*. The early scenes are wrought with such astounding skill that although Macbeth meditates the crime of murder itself upon one who is his sovereign, his guest, his benefactor, a virtuous man aged and asleep, we yet hold our breath in fear lest he should not accomplish his design. We are all on Macbeth's side, and look with cold hostility upon the good men and true who hold him in suspicion after the crime is discovered. This is a miracle of craftsmanship, but its success makes it all the harder to secure our hearty applause for the destruction of the usurper at the end. To meet the need, Shakespeare gives us a brief scene, most unwisely omitted in some modern representations—the butchery of Macduff's wife and splendid little son. This concentration of pathos, horror, shame, and villainy brings mercilessly before us the meaning to Scotland of Macbeth's dominion; it is forced violently upon our gaze, and we sicken. In a companion scene this is brought to bear—the announcement to Macduff and his friends. One notes in passing how the two passages are stuck deep into our minds by what can only be called the ferocious quaintness of the language—" What, you egg! Young fry of treachery! " and

> What, all my pretty chickens and their dam
> At one fell swoop ?—

words that even amid the gorgeous language of the whole tragedy cannot be forgotten. So it is that when Macduff, not Malcolm (for we have not actually witnessed the murder of Duncan, his father), at length faces the tyrant, all our sympathy is found to have deserted Macbeth for his adversary.

Equal skill is put forth by Æschylus in *Agamemnon*, or, more exactly, in the trilogy of which that drama is the first part. Throughout most of *Agamemnon* the playwright wishes us to see events from Clytæmnestra's point of view, although she treacherously murders her husband, on his triumphant return from Troy, in order to be free for Ægisthus and to share Agamemnon's throne with him. Therefore not only is her husband represented as cold, arrogant, shallow; the outrage he inflicted years ago upon his wife by slaying their daughter Iphigeneia is time and again mentioned, above all in an unspeakably beautiful and pathetic lyrical narrative. Again, although the Queen has a lover, through all the terrible scenes of her own plotting and crime she stands alone, while Agamemnon's unwilling concubine Cassandra is exhibited by him with careless brutality to his wife and to the whole city. Thus everything is done to secure our sympathy for Clytæmnestra. But when this tragedy is over, we are to pass at once to *The Libation-Bearers*, wherein Orestes avenges his royal father by slaying the murderess, his own mother, and retains our sympathy even while so acting. If this sympathy is to be possible every available device is clearly needed. Accordingly we find Orestes impelled to his frightful task, not only by desire to avenge his father and seize the usurped sceptre, but by the unmistakable fiat of the Most High and by appalling threats in the event of disobedience. But the special point we have now in mind is this. Just as we are about to enter upon *The Libation-Bearers*, at the close of *Agamem-*

non, we are prepared for the necessary swing-round of sympathy by the entrance of Ægisthus, Clytæmnestra's paramour, who sums up in his own person all the evil of which the Queen is guilty, everything which can rouse our hostility against her. Had he appeared in the earlier scenes, the atmosphere and tone which Æschylus there needed would have been impossible. The poet introduces him not too soon, and just in time.

Each of these three great phases, complication, catastrophe, and *dénouement,* is exposed to a peculiar and special danger. It is enough here to remind the reader of that which threatens the second phase. We have already shown that those catastrophes are bad which are obtruded on us with no warning at all—the *deus ex machina,* or " Uncle Peter " as we called him.

The commonest weakness of complication-scenes (" First Acts ") is an over-developed medley of incidents and minor characters, which offer a number of false trails and prevent us from seeing as early as we should what the problem or question is. Ancient drama, by its very nature as " classical " work, contains no instance of this; but for the analogous reason it is fairly common in modern drama. Such a bushy beginning is to be found in M. Henri Lavedan's *Viveurs*. This is an admirably vigorous picture of many people whose interests clash or entwine themselves together, but all is detailed and minor; only late in the play do we fully realize that it is Mme. Blandin's emotional experience and development which provide the structure. But it is significant that spectators of the presentation found far less difficulty, since the rôle of Mme. Blandin was played by one of the most celebrated actresses in the world, Mme. Réjane. A similar vagueness, but sooner dispelled, marks the opening of Mr. Granville Barker's *The Madras House* : Huxtable's daughters are so numerous and so talkative that, while one admires the dreadful verisimilitude of the household, one wonders (as the phrase goes) " what it is all about." This quality is often to be remarked in Russian drama, not excluding Tchekof's celebrated *Cherry Orchard*. Or we may go much further and assert that the Russian playwrights tend to employ this " bushiness " from beginning to end of a play; construction melts into atmosphere, foreground merges into background. This applies to some English work influenced by the Russian vogue; for example, Mr. Shaw's *Heartbreak House*, which formally claims to be "a Fantasia in the Russian manner on English themes," is certainly justified of its pretensions. It does indeed possess a plot which can be stated, but the plot is well-nigh overgrown by a jungle of little happenings, minor exits and entrances, and unrelated controversies which exist only to convey atmosphere.

Much more needs to be said about *dénouement*; and before we discuss its besetting danger, let us point to a feature which is fairly common in our time and which has been mistakenly censured. This feature has often been described by the remark: "The curtain descends upon a note of interrogation." It may seem clear that, if the concluding phase should provide a "solution," nothing could well be worse than to end with a question, a difficulty unsettled. But here is a misunderstanding. The "last act" must solve the original complication, but it may itself, without any breach whatsoever of artistic perfection, contain a question or actually consist of one. The reader will recall a familiar joke. "Is it true that you Americans always answer one question with another?" "Do we?" Take the finale of *A Doll's House*. It matters nothing that we end with a breach between husband and wife which may or may not be closed and the possibility of closing which is actually mooted by them. That breach, however important, is no flaw in the dramatic structure; nay, it is necessary to the solution. The *dénouement* demanded by the earlier scenes is certainly not a new *modus vivendi* arranged by the illuminated Torvald and Nora. Neither is yet competent to suggest any really satisfying and sound basis of married life; indeed Nora's spiritual immaturity is again and again pressed upon us—it is this which involves her with Krogstad, this which alone justifies the tarantella dance and the macaroons. No; the poet has carefully and justly restricted the *dénouement* to this, that Nora's eyes are completely opened to the conditions of her married life, and that she insists on understanding things better than she does before continuing to live with her husband; the "question" is an integral and vital part of the solution. Again, in the *Rhesus* attributed to Euripides, it is not clear, from the play itself, whether the Trojans, when they arm at the close, are going forth to victory or disaster; but that does not imply any futility at all in the dramatic form, since the question set by the tragedy is only this: What will result from the unexpected arrival of Rhesus to succour Troy? It has been objected against Mr. Barker's play, *The Voysey Inheritance*, that we cannot tell, when the curtain falls, whether young Edward Voysey will be exposed and ruined or not. This, again, matters nothing to the plot, which is concerned, not with his social repute or wealth, but only with the question: How will he face the strange responsibility fixed upon him by his father? He accepts it with all its consequences; what the danger actually brings to him is not the point, and Mr. Barker has shown admirable artistic boldness in leaving unanswered an irrelevant question—to answer it would have been to blur the issue.

The danger which does beset the solution-stage of the play is utterly different; it is an irrational simplicity, or rather simplification, the adoption of improper short cuts in order to end matters quickly, neatly, completely. The reason for this seems to be that the playwright has misconceived the nature of a dramatic ending; he inclines to confuse climax, catastrophe, peripeteia, with conclusion, *dénouement,* solution. As we have seen, the catastrophe does not properly solve the problem, but provides a method of, or means to, a solution; thereafter follows, or should follow, a phase equally needed, the working-out of the solution. *Œdipus Tyrannus* affords an excellent example of this difference, but there are naturally many such masterpieces. In *Man and Superman* Mr. Shaw produces a fine catastrophe in Ann's avowal of her love to John Tanner; but how he will meet this crisis is a new question, and (in view of the character and opinions which he has revealed) a question fraught with deep interest. In *The Brothers*, by Terence, the climax (we saw) is Demea's decision to change his manners. This forms anything but a conclusion or solution: we look with excited amusement to see how this resolve will affect the two young men and the elderly Micio whom Demea has at length decided to beat at his own game. *Julius*

Cæsar contains a very long elaborate *dénouement* which no one could conceivably confuse with the peripeteia. In Molière's *Le Misanthrope* the peripeteia is of course the scene where the coquette Célimène is at length " brought to book " by the production of her hopelessly damaging letter in the presence of her various suitors. But no reader or spectator can tell whether this will or will not throw her finally into the arms of Alceste; in fact the conclusion is probably felt by most as a shock.

But instances need not be multiplied; any good play distinguishes climax and conclusion. Only bad writers entirely confuse them; nevertheless, competent playwrights do at times incline towards such confusion. But we must beware of bringing under this head plays with a *dénouement* which is brief, or less interesting than the climax or perhaps than any of the earlier scenes, as in many light comedies, such as Mr. Arnold Bennett's *The Honeymoon*. The fault we have in view is the idea that after the peripeteia there is nothing to do save to " pick up the pieces "—the audience knows and understands everything; let us simply square things up and ring down the curtain.

So it comes to pass that the characters forget their own natures, drop the purposes which have sustained them hitherto, reveal ludicrously casual forgetfulness or generosity, in order to put everything " straight." Thus at the close of *Cymbeline*, so as to get rid of the war with Rome which might disturb the spectators amid the joy caused by all the personal reconciliations, the King glibly utters this incredible announcement :—

> And, Caius Lucius,
> Although the victor, we submit to Cæsar,
> And to the Roman empire, promising
> To pay our wonted tribute, from the which
> We were dissuaded by our wicked queen :
> Whom heavens, in justice, both on her and hers,
> Have laid most heavy hand.

This calm assumption, conceived by a British king, that Heaven willed the subjection of Britain to Rome so definitely as to make patriotism a species of impiety—an assumption which would be out of the question in the body of any play, whether composed by Shakespeare or by the completest dunce— is a first-rate example of what we may term the " huddled " ending. It would be difficult to find elsewhere quite such perfect rubbish, but the lapse in technique is common. Euripides' *Alcestis* provides at the close not only no account of the manner in which Heracles rescued the Queen from the Death-fiend (an omission which may well have a vital bearing on the whole plot), but no conversation or real contact between Admetus and his restored wife. In *Monsieur Piégois*, by M. Alfred Capus, Piégois not only relinquishes his career as director of the casino, but gives the whole concern over to the town, for no discoverable reason save to create an amiable sensation in the theatre. St. John Hankin, too, sinned grievously in *The Two Mr. Wetherbys*. The whole point of Richard Wetherby is his humorous but adamantine resolve not to come back to his wife. The plot is built on this, but at the last moment, though no new factor has appeared, he collapses, simply for the sake of a good "curtain"—to produce a neat tableau of two couples instead of one couple *plus* two isolated persons; it is the cheapest theatricality, and a most curious phenomenon in this author, who expressed himself later very strongly against the mechanical "happy ending," and in such an admirable drama as *The Last of the de Mullins* achieved a capital solution. "Huddled" scenes are indeed usually employed to secure a " happy ending," as in the numberless Elizabethan plays where incongruous and unsuspecting minor persons are hastily betrothed by an unscrupulous dramatist. The Duke in *Twelfth Night* at the last minute turns unaccountably to Viola from Olivia; at the end of *A Winter's Tale*, Camillo and Paulina become affianced without having shown any hint of such interest in one another—simply because it *is* the end of *A Winter's Tale*, not the beginning; Isabella's acceptance of the Duke in *Measure for Measure* is still worse. These absurd nuptials, and a hundred more, are poverty-stricken devices to secure that crispness of action which should depend on sanely-developed psychology, not on a feverish hustle less appropriate to a clear-headed artist than to a traveller who wildly packs a portmanteau just in time for his train. Oscar Wilde's cynical attitude towards the stage was never revealed more pungently than when at the close of *The Importance of Being Earnest* he bade Miss Prism and the Canon fall into one another's arms without the shadow of excuse or warning. The conclusion of *The Merchant of Venice* is in this respect highly curious. The peripeteia is, of course, the sudden ruling that Shylock must take no more and no less than exactly one pound of flesh. The *dénouement* (properly so called) is not the whole of what follows, namely part of the Fourth, and the whole of the Fifth, Act; that portion of the drama contains the genuine *dénouement* and more. For the problem of the play is : What will result from Shylock's hatred against Antonio ? The *dénouement* as usual gives the answer by aid of the peripeteia : Shylock is utterly baffled, while Antonio receives both life and money to compensate his losses at sea. Therefore the play might have ended with the close of the Trial Scene, and assuredly the Fifth Act, delightful as it is and containing as it does some of the most marvellous poetry that even Shakespeare ever penned, strikes us all as a kind of appendix; we hardly feel that it is needed. We should regard it still more definitely as intrusive had not the playwright mechanically inserted a few hooks in the Fourth Act whereon to hang it, notably the brief scene where the supposed advocate and clerk coax Bassanio and Gratiano into surrendering their rings. Further, we are prepared for the scene of Lorenzo and Jessica by Antonio's insistence before the court that Shylock be compelled to provide for them. All this seems anything but a huddled ending; it shows on the contrary a quite languid development. There is nevertheless a short huddled passage concerned with the main plot. Antonio is to be fully restored, and so Portia suddenly thrusts at him certain letters—how she came by them we are left to guess—which report that all his supposedly lost ships are "safely come to land."

A moment ago we used the phrase "main plot." It might seem from our discussion of plot that the term is self-contradictory. But secondary or minor plots of course abound. Are they legitimate? This question is not so troublesome as might appear. An "under-plot" is always interesting and complete in itself (else it would not be a plot at all) but it may and should support the main action. Just so an Æschylean play can be read—now, unfortunately, must as a rule be read—and appreciated in itself; but on studying the whole trilogy we perceive that it forms part of a still greater organism. The by-play of Trinculo and Stephano is valuable as bringing out the nature of Caliban and so strengthening our appreciation of Prospero. But if the two plots are essentially separate and are only tied together by some thin device, for example, by the fact that the same character happens, and merely happens, to take part in both, then the minor plot is technically improper. It may be magnificent in itself —the Falstaff scenes of *Henry IV.*, Part I., fall under this category—but it is a flaw in the whole drama as a drama. We are, in short, presented with two plays instead of one. We may say, if we choose, that the discussion deals purely with technical labels; but on the other side let us not deny that no one can recollect the whole action of *Henry IV.*, Part I., of *A Midsummer Night's Dream*, of *Cymbeline*, without two entirely distinct mental processes, exactly as the reader of Dickens finds it an effort to remember that Mrs. Gamp and Mr. Elijah Pogram appear between the covers of the same novel.

It may prove useful, before bringing this essay to an end, to discuss a few among the many misconceptions which have helped to confuse popular opinion and even professional criticism — misuse of words and incorrect doctrines. "Dramatic" is a term often wrongly applied. People think of drama, not as a certain form of art, but as what they have been accustomed to see in a theatre. Now, the majority of successful plays in our time (to mention no other) have been less strong in genuine dramatic art than in theatricality—that is, a vivid picture of bustle, violence, excitement, a falsetto note of vague momentousness. Play after play has been presented which is derived, not from life or any direct thought about life, but from imitation of the last piece which has won applause. Hence that artificial heightening and stressing, those sudden entrances and exits, those French windows, those "strong curtains," all the *va-et-vient* of alternate emotions with which every one is so familiar, and which—here is the deadly point—form the only scenic pabulum available in the vast majority of provincial towns. Then, what is merely theatrical is dubbed "dramatic"; any occasion when one feels that "something is going to happen" is given this adjective. An important criminal case is called "dramatic" because the black cap lies on the judge's table, or because a Cabinet Minister is a witness—that is, we experience the appetizing thrill which a pretentious stage-spectacle affords. The judge's rebuke has even become a jocular proverb: "This court is not a theatre." As a fact, a murder case may be utterly undramatic, and a trial which centres round a sordid theft may be full of drama, as Mr. Galsworthy has admirably demonstrated. Another abused word is "tragedy," incessantly applied by journalists to any violent death, apparently because in so many real tragedies the chief person loses his life. It will naturally be so, since this is the easiest way to communicate a sense of solemnity and to strip the disguise from people and situations. But even if a tragedy always contained a death (which is not true) it by no means follows that every death, even violent death, is tragic. It must involve not only a human life, but also the victory, defeat, or rescue of some idea important to human beings. But in newspaper jargon, if a pauper dies just before news of sudden wealth reaches him, or if a child is killed by an overdose of medicine, these events are called tragedies. Pitiful they are, but not (as reported) tragic in the least; there is far more of tragedy in the death of a bird, if it means what Ibsen's wild duck means. So debased is our use of words that a few years ago a newspaper remarked concerning certain deaths from disease: "Some of these tragedies are dramatic"! A third misused term is "catastrophe." Critics have been known to apply it loosely to the conclusion of a drama, thus mischievously confusing climax or peripeteia with *dénouement*. Far more frequent is the implication of "disaster," mostly (it is true) about real and non-dramatic events, such as a fatal shipwreck, but sometimes of a disastrous event in the course of a play, which is not a real catastrophe in the least, such as Cæsar's murder, or the death of Alcestis.

Few doctrines are more frequently expressed than this, that tragedy, or even comedy, shows Man in conflict with Fate, or Circumstance, as it is sometimes called. One hears a good deal about "puppets of Fate," and Mr. Thomas Hardy plainly imagines himself to have derived from Æschylus a point of view which, though it leaves his works unimpaired as magnificent works of art, does make them at times grossly unfair pictures of the Divine Government; namely, his idea that the dice are always cogged in favour of sorrow, waste, misunderstanding, that accident is invariably unhappy accident. Such a doctrine can be attributed to Æschylus only by a grave mistake. And as regards the general proposition, it is possible to regard drama as depicting Man's struggle against Fate only if we dilute " Fate " until all definite meaning vanishes. What a playwright ultimately believes as a religious or metaphysical fact is one thing; what he actually adduces as the initial point of his play is another. And he always thus adduces a specific situation clearly attributable to the circumscribed acts, hopes, and fears of *people*, not to any arrangement of the Universe; even in the *Prometheus* we are concerned with a purely personal Zeus.

It is a common theory that dramatists should present us with "a slice of life." Two errors are here combined: that drama imitates life, and that the author cuts off a portion from a real sequence of events and stages it without more ado. The latter idea need not detain us. It is plain that a dramatist organizes his material, giving to it structure and lucidity, emphasizing tendencies only latent in actual affairs, and omitting the irrelevant. But that he imitates life may seem a more attractive theory. His real task, however, is not to imitate but to interpret, and the semblance of actuality is but the beginning of the work. Constable represented the Glebe Farm accurately, no doubt, but his painting will never be mistaken for a coloured photograph. Similarly, the most realistic of playwrights may vividly present a quarrel or a conspiracy, but he is transmuting in the very moment at which we cry, "How natural!" —he gives text and comment in one breath, which is the method of all art.

Finally, the most famous of all theories concerning the drama may be dismissed in few words. It was long claimed that tragedy should follow the "classical" style and conform to the Three Unities, of Action, Time, and Place, because Aristotle in his *Poetic* has so ordained. Not only is it possible to reply that Aristotle's "rules" do not bind human activity for ever, not only is it obvious to point out that, in all his "rules," he is manifestly doing no more than to codify the practice of Greek playwrights in his own and earlier times; much more than all this, it is the bald truth—though it is difficult to believe it, for this celebrated "rule" has been repeated for centuries and has cramped French tragedy in the hands of great masters—it is the truth that Aristotle never mentions the "Three Unities." He insists, naturally, on the importance of unity in action, and makes one passing remark that it is advisable to restrict the events of a drama to one revolution of the sun, but has not a word on the "Unity of Place," which is signally violated in the *Eumenides* of Æschylus, the *Ajax* of Sophocles, and in several of Aristophanes' comedies. The "Three Unities" are the greatest imposture in the history of criticism.

INDEX OF PLACES

Æ. =Æschylus, Ar. =Aristophanes, B. =Barker, E. =Euripides,
G. =Galsworthy, H. =Hankin, I. =Ibsen, M. =Molière,
P. =Pinero, S. =Sophocles, Sh. =Shakespeare, W. =Wilde

Ægean Sea, 41
Argos, 17, 41
Athens, 5–6, 38–9, 44, 46
— and Persia, 5–6
Aulis, 16

Belmont, 140
Birmingham, Repertory theatres in, 107
Birnam Wood, 178
Brighton, 87
Britain, 43, 50, 198

Cathay, 5
Christchurch, Oxford, 66
Colchis, 30
Copenhagen, 52
Corinth, 30, 35

Dakota, 31
Dublin, 107
Dunsinane, 141, 178

Eastcheap, 140
England, 1–2, 3, 5, 49, 57, 124; in the nineteenth century, 3
Europe, 4

Fife, 167
Forest of Arden, 141

Gadshill, 117
Gaul, 43
Germany, Ibsen in, 52, 56
Glasgow, 107
Greece, 11, 41

Hades, in Ar. *Frogs*, 47, 184
Hampton Court, 141

Iolchos, 29
Ireland, 4

London, 3, 52, 107–8

Monte Carlo, 66
Mycenæ, 24

New South Wales, 164
Nile, 141

Persia, 5–6, 185–6
Phthia, 19

Queensland, 31

Rialto, The, 188
Rome, 124, 188

Salamis, 185
Scandinavia, I.'s plays in, 52
Scotland, 4, 188
Sipylus, 19
Spain, 43
Sparta, and King of Sparta, 40
Stratford-on-Avon, 141

Thebes, 178
Thessaly, 43
Troy, 16, 18, 20, 24, 40, 41–2, 189, 195
Tuileries, 73

Wales, 4
Waterloo, 181

INDEX OF PERSONS AND WORKS

Names of authors in small capitals, of works in italics

Abraham Lincoln, see DRINKWATER
Acharnians, The, see ARISTOPHANES
Achilles, in E. *I. at A.*, 16 ff., 41; speech of, trans., 18 ff.
Achurch, Miss Janet, 52
Admetus, 130, 199
Admirable Crichton, The, see BARRIE
Ægisthus, in Æ. *Agam.*, 189–91; in E. *Electra*, 24, 26 f.
ÆSCHYLUS, 25, 47, 146, 147, 148, 189 ff.
— and HARDY, 206
— in Ar. *Frogs*, 184
— *Agamemnon*, 133, 154, 189 ff.
— *Choephoræ*, 150, 170
— *Eumenides*, 209
— *Persæ*, catastrophe of, 185 f.
— *Prometheus Vinctus*, 150, 207; economy in, 169; peripeteia in, 177
— *Supplices*, 170
— *The Libation-Bearers* (=*Choeph.*), 190 ff.
Agamemnon, in Æ. *Ag.*, 189 f.; in E. *Electra*, 17 ff., 24 ff.
Agamemnon, see ÆSCHYLUS
Ajax, see SOPHOCLES
Alceste, in M. *Le Misanthrope*, 150, 176, 197
Alcestis, in E. *Alc.*, 130, 199, 206
Alcestis, see EURIPIDES
Alice in Wonderland, 67
Anatol, see SCHNITZLER
ANDERSEN, HANS, 140
ANDREIEV, *The Sabine Women*, 133
Androcles and the Lion, see SHAW

Andromache, in E. *Andr.*, 40
Andromache, see EURIPIDES
Antigone, see SOPHOCLES
Antonio, in Sh. *M. of V.*, 75–6, 168, 187–8, 201–2
Antony, Mark, in Sh. *J. C.*, 136, 140; his funeral speech, 156, 182
Antony and Cleopatra, see SHAKESPEARE
Apollo, in E. *Electra*, 24
ARCHER, MR. WILLIAM, 52; his *Playmaking*, 112 n.; (pp. 23–41), 145 n.
Are You a Mason ? 152
ARISTOPHANES, 11, 148
— and EURIPIDES, 45 ff.
— and the "Three Unities," 209
— his comedy often passes into farce, 120–1
— *Acharnians*, 183
— *Birds*, 184
— *Frogs*, 46; peripeteia in, 177, 184
— *Peace*, 184
— *Plutus*, 183
ARISTOTLE, 162; and the "Three Unities," 208–9; on irrational elements in drama, 130; on plot, 144; on slaves, 33
ARISTOTLE'S canons, 53; *desis*, 132; peripeteia, 175
— rule of plot-construction, 174
Arms and the Man, see SHAW
Artemis, 17, 41, 168
As You Like It, see SHAKESPEARE
Athena, in E., 45
Atreus, sons of, in E. *I. at A.*, 18

INDEX OF PERSONS AND WORKS 213

Audrey, in Sh. *As You*, 170
AUGIER, *La Pierre de Touche*, 153
Avariés, Les, see BRIEUX

Bacchæ, see EURIPIDES
Back to Methuselah, see SHAW
BAILLIE, JOANNA, 49
Banquo, 167
BARKER, MR. GRANVILLE, 52, 60, 74, 86 ff., 106, 173, 195
—— *Prunella*, 86
—— *The Madras House*, 86, 90 ff., 154, 192
—— *The Marrying of Ann Leete*, 71, 87–8, 93
—— *The Voysey Inheritance*, 88–9, 93, 195–6
—— *Waste*, 89–90
BARRIE, SIR J. M., 67
—— *Mary Rose*, 174
—— *Peter Pan*, 67, 163
—— *The Admirable Crichton*, 67
Bartholomew Fair, see JONSON
Bassanio, in Sh. *M. of V.*, 168, 201
Belvidera, in Otway's *V. Pres.*, 181
BENNETT, MR. ARNOLD, 67; his " sense of the theatre," 67
—— *Milestones*, 67
—— *The Honeymoon*, 67; peripeteia in, 197
—— *The Title*, 67
Bernadotte, 134
BESIER, MR. RUDOLF, 64; *Don*, 64
Birds, The, see ARISTOPHANES
Blanco Posnet, see SHAW
Blandin, Mme., in Lavedan's *Viveurs*, 192
Bloomfield Bonnington, Sir Ralph, in Shaw, *Dr.'s Dil.*, 16
Bluntschli, in Shaw, *A. and M.*, 11, 150, 169
Borridge, Ethel, in H. *Cass. Eng.*, 79
BOTTOMLEY, MR. GORDON, 59
BOUCICAULT, DION, 49, 160–1

Boy, The, see PINERO
Brack, Judge, in I. *H. G.*, 167
Bracknell, Lord, in W. *Import.*, 60
BRADLEY, PROFESSOR A. C., 142 ; his *Shakespearean Tragedy*, 115 n.
Brassbound, Captain, in Shaw, 26
BRIEUX, M., 106, 125
Brothers, The, see TERENCE
BROWNING, 59
Burglar Who Failed, The, see HANKIN
Burgoyne, General, in Shaw, *Devil's D.*, 14–5

Cæsar, in Sh. *Cymb.*, 198
—— in Sh. *J. C.*, 206
Cæsar and Cleopatra, see SHAW
Cæsar, Julius, his landing in Britain, 110
—— —— in Shaw, *C. and Cl.*, 42, 97–8
Cairn, David, in Mrs. *G.'s Necklace*, 152
Caius Lucius, in Sh. *Cymb.*, 198
Calchas, in E. *I. at A.*, 17, 19
CALDERON, GEORGE, 60, 71, 104 ff.
Camillo, in Sh. *A W.'s T.*, 200
Candida, see SHAW
Capulets and Montagues, in Sh. *R. and J.*, 158
CAPUS, M. ALFRED, *M. Piégois*, 132, 199
Carlyle, 4
Cassandra, in Æ. *Agam.*, 190
Cassilis Engagement, The, see HANKIN
—— Geoffrey, in H. *The C. Eng.*, 79
Cassio, in Sh. *Oth.*, 136
Cassius, in Sh. *J. C.*, 136
Caste, see ROBERTSON
Cecily, Lady, in Shaw, *Capt. B.*, 23
Célimène, in M. *Le Misan.*, 150, 197
Chantecler, see ROSTAND

214   EURIPIDES AND SHAW

Charity that began at Home, The, see HANKIN
Charmian, in Sh. *A. and Cl.*, 170
Charrington, Mr. Charles, 52
Charteris, in Shaw, *Philand.*, 101
Cherry Orchard, see TCHEKOF
Chiron, mentioned in E. *I. at A.*, 18.
Chremes, in Terence, *Phormio*, 185
Cleon, 45, 47
Cleopatra, in Sh. *A. and C.*, 136, 140
Clytæmnestra, 17, 20, 189 ff.
CONGREVE, 60, 103, 149
Constable, 208
Constant Lover, The, see HANKIN
Coriolanus, see SHAKESPEARE
Course du Flambeau, see HERVIEU
COURTNEY, MR. W. L., 69
Critic, The, see SHERIDAN
Crusoe, Robinson, see DEFOE
Cusins, in Shaw, *Maj. B.*, 101
Cymbeline, see SHAKESPEARE

Dane's Defence, Mrs., 187, see JONES
Darius, 186
Darlington, Lord, in W. *Ly. W.'s Fan*, 61
David Garrick, 49
DAVIES, MR. H. H., *Mrs. Gorringe's Necklace*, 152
DEFOE, DANIEL, *Robinson Crusoe*, has no plot, 112 ff.
Demea, in Ter. *Brothers*, 185, 196
Denison, Lady, in H. *Charity*, 78
Desdemona, 154, 167
Devil's Disciple, The, see SHAW
DICKENS, 3, 49, 101
Dionysus, 184
Divine Gift, The, see JONES
Doctor's Dilemma, The, see SHAW
Doll's House, A, see IBSEN
Don, see BESIER
Don Juan in Hell, see SHAW

Doyle, Larry, in Shaw, *Jo. B.*, 104
Drama and Life, see WALKLEY
Dramatic Values, see MONTAGUE
DRINKWATER, MR. JOHN, *Abraham Lincoln*, 135
Dubedat, Louis, in Shaw, *Dr.'s Dil.*, 9
Dudgeon, Dick, in Shaw, *Devil's D.*, 96, 99
— Mrs., in Shaw, *Devil's D.*, 16
DUMAS *fils, Francillon*, 169
Duncan, in Sh. *Macb.*, 167, 175, 181, 189

Eldest Son, The, see GALSWORTHY
Electra, in E. *El.*, 24 ff.
Electra, see EURIPIDES
Elizabeth, 138
Elmire, in M. *Tartuffe*, 184
Emilia, in Sh. *Oth.*, 136
Enemy of the People, An, see IBSEN
Enobarbus, in Sh. *A. and C.*, 136
Erlynne, Mrs., in W. *Ly. W.'s Fan*, 180
ERVINE, MR. ST. JOHN, 115 n.
Eugene Marchbanks, in Shaw, *Cand.*, 103
EURIPIDES, 1–48 *passim*, 146 ff., 158, 170
— in Ar. *Frogs*, 184
— *Alcestis*, 34, 197 ; accident in, 130
— *Andromache*, 34, 39, 40
— *Bacchæ*, 10–1 (qd. in trans.)
— *Electra*, 24 ff.
— *Hecuba*, economy in, 169
— *Helena*, 119
— *Hippolytus*, 34, 168, 190
— *Iphigenia at Aulis*, 16 ff., 41–2
— *Medea*, 29 ff., 31, 123, 135, 150
— *Orestes*, 118, 170
— *Rhesus*, 194
Eustace, in H. *Prodigal*, 81
Every Man out of his Humour, see JONSON

INDEX OF PERSONS AND WORKS 215

Falstaff, in Sh., 140, 182; in *Hy. IV.*, 117, 140, 168, 203; in Sh. *M. Wives*, 138
Faust, 111, 175
Faust, see GOETHE
Felicia Hindemarsh, in Jones, *Mrs. D.'s Def.*, 180
Ferrand, in G. *Pigeon*, 81
Ferrovius, in Shaw, *Andr.*, 100
FIELDING, HENRY, 49
Fontenais, Mme., in Hervieu, *La C. du Fl.*, 151
Fool, in Sh. *Lear*, 151
Forbes-Robertson, Sir Johnston, 97
Fountain, The, see CALDERON
Francillon, see DUMAS
Friar Laurence, in Sh. *R. and J.*, 128, 158 (qd.)
Friday, Man, in *R. Crusoe*, 107
Frogs, The, see ARISTOPHANES
Froufrou, see MEILHAC-HALÉVY

GALSWORTHY, MR. JOHN, 60, 71, 74, 80 ff., 105, 205
—— *Justice*, 84–5, 125
—— *Strife*, 154
—— *The Eldest Son*, 81
—— *The Pigeon*, 81–2 (qd.)
—— *The Silver Box*, 82 ff.
—— *The Skin Game*, 85
Gamp, Mrs., 203
Garnett, Miss, in Shaw, *Candida*, 103
Garrick, David, 49
George Dandin, see MOLIÈRE
Getting Married, see SHAW
Ghosts, see IBSEN
Gloria, in Shaw, *You Never*, 101
GOETHE, *Faust*, 122, 147 (qd.)
Gorringe's Necklace, Mrs., see DAVIES
Grant, General, 111
Gratiano, in Sh. *M. of V.*, 201
Grieg, 133
Guinea-Hen, in Rostand, *Chantecler*, 153

Hal, Prince, in Sh. *Hy. IV.*, 168
Hallam, Sir Howard, in Shaw, *Capt. B.*, 16, 22 ff., 26

Hamlet, in Sh. *H.*, 111, 115 n., 142 ff., 182
Hamlet, see SHAKESPEARE
HANKIN, ST. JOHN, 60, 71, 76 ff., 81, 105–6
—— *The Burglar who failed*, 76
—— *The Cassilis Engagement*, 76, 79
—— *The Charity that began at Home*, 76, 78–9
—— *The Constant Lover*, 76
—— *The Last of the de Mullins*, 76, 79–80, 199
—— *The Return of the Prodigal*, 76 ff., 80
—— *The Two Mr. Wetherbys*, 76–7, 199
HARDY, MR. THOMAS, and Æ., 206
—— *Tess of the D'Urbervilles*, 75
—— *The Return of the Native*, 93
Harpagon, in M. *L'Avare*, 141–2
HAUPTMANN, 158
Heartbreak House, see SHAW
Hector, 40
Hecuba, see EURIPIDES
Hedda Gabler, see IBSEN
Hedwig, in I. *W. Duck*, 76
HEINE, 183
Helen, mentioned in E. *I. at A.*, 41
Helena, see EURIPIDES
Helmer, Nora, in I. *Doll's H.*, 56, 131, 180, 194
— Torvald, in I. *Doll's H.*, 56, 131, 180, 194
Henry the Fifth, in Sh. *Hy. V.*, 175
Henry the Fifth, see SHAKESPEARE
Henry the Fourth, see SHAKESPEARE
Henry the Sixth, see SHAKESPEARE
Hepplewhite, 106
Heracles, in Æ. *Prom. V.*, 169; in E. *Alc.*, 130, 199
Heralds, in Æ. *Supplices*, etc., 170

Herdsman, in S. *Œ. Tyr.*, 178
HERVIEU, 158; *La Course du Flambeau* (qd.), 151
Hill, Jenny, in Shaw, *Maj. B.*, 44
Hippolytus, see EURIPIDES
Hobbyhorse, The, 53; see PINERO
Honeymoon, The, see BENNETT
Hotspur, in Sh. *Hy. IV.*, 140
HOUSMAN, MR. LAURENCE, 86
How He Lied to her Husband, see SHAW
Huxtable family, in B. *Madras H.*, 90, 92, 192

Iago, in Sh. *Oth.*, 136-7, 167
IBSEN, 50, 53 ff., 62, 69, 95, 101, 106-7, 136, 148, 158, etc. etc.
— chief aim of, 54, 124
— dialogue in, 162
— his influence on English playwrights, etc., 59, 64, 173
— *A Doll's House*, 49, 52, 55, 128, 131, 179, 194
— *An Enemy of the People*, 52, 57, 172-3
— *Ghosts*, 54, 56 ff.
— *Hedda Gabler*, 53-4, 58, 136-7, 147, 163, 167-8
— *Little Eyolf*, 154
— *Peer Gynt*, 163
— *Rosmersholm*, 52
— *The Master Builder*, 136
— *The Wild Duck*, 52, 58, 76, 136, 206
Idea of Tragedy, The, see COURTNEY
Importance of Being Earnest, The, see WILDE
Io, in Æ. *Prom. V.*, 169
Iphigenia at Aulis, see EURIPIDES
Isabella, in Sh. *Meas. for M.*, 200

Jack Straw, see MAUGHAM
Jacob, mentioned in Sh. *M. of V.*, 75
Jaffier, in Otway, *Venice Pres.*, 181

Jason, in E. *Medea*, 28 ff., 36
Jessica, in Sh. *M. of V.*, 202
Jocasta, in S. *Œ. Tyr.*, 178
John Bull's Other Island, see SHAW
JONES, MR. HENRY ARTHUR, 60, 67-8, 173
— — *Michael and his Lost Angel*, 68
— — *Mrs. Dane's Defence*, 180
— — *The Divine Gift*, 68
— — *The Liars*, 68
— — *The Philistines*, 68
Jones, in G. *Silver Box*, 83
JONSON, BEN, 149
Jourdain, M., 154
Julia, in Shaw, *Philand.*, 101
Juliet, in Sh. *R. and J.*, 128
Juliet's nurse, in Sh. *R. and J.*, 171
Julius Cæsar, in Sh. *J. C.*, 135, 181
Julius Cæsar, see SHAKESPEARE
Justice, see GALSWORTHY

KEATS, 72
Kent, in Sh. *Lear*, 151
King Lear, see SHAKESPEARE
Krogstad, in I. *D.'s Ho.*, 128, 131, 194
KYD, *The Spanish Tragedy*, a good melodrama, 119

Laban, 75
Lady Windermere's Fan, see WILDE
Laius, in S. *Œ. Tyr.*, 178
Lamachus, in Ar. *Ach.*, 183
Land of Promise, The, see MAUGHAM
La Pierre de Touche, see AUGIER
LA ROCHEFOUCAULD, 161
Last of the de Mullins, The, see HANKIN
LAVEDAN, M. HENRI, *Viveurs*, 192
Lavinia, in Shaw, *Andro.*, 100
Liars, The, see JONES
Libation-Bearers, The, see ÆSCHYLUS

INDEX OF PERSONS AND WORKS 217

Linden, Mrs., in I. *D.'s Ho.*, 128, 131
Little Eyolf, see IBSEN
London Assurance, see BOUCICAULT
LONGFELLOW, 104
Lorenzo, in Sh. *M. of V.*, 202
Louka, in Shaw, *A. and M.*, 169
Love and Mr. Lewisham, see WELLS

MACAULAY, 3–4
Macbeth, in Sh. *Macb.*, 113, 115 n., 142, 150, 167, 175, 178, 182, 188–9
— his soliloquies, 156
— Lady, in Sh. *Macb.*, 140, 150
Macbeth, see SHAKESPEARE
Macduff, 188 f.
Madras, Constantine, in B. *M. House*, 90
Madras House, The, see BARKER
MAETERLINCK, M., 74; dialogue in, 155
Magistrate, The, see PINERO
Major Barbara, see SHAW
Mak, in the *Secunda Pastorum* "Towneley" Miracle-Play, 112
Malcolm, in Sh. *Macb.*, 189
Man and Superman, see SHAW
Man in the Stalls, The, see SUTRO
Man of Destiny, The, see SHAW
Marchbanks, Eugene, in Shaw, *Candida*, 103
MARIVAUX, 121
Marrying of Ann Leete, The, see BARKER
MARSTON, WESTLAND, 49, 61, 107
Mary Rose, see BARRIE
MASEFIELD, MR. JOHN, 60, 71
Master Builder, The, see IBSEN
MAUGHAM, MR. SOMERSET, 66; *Jack Straw*, 66; *The Land of Promise*, 67
Maximes et Réflexions Morales, of LA ROCHEFOUCAULD, 161

Measure for Measure, see SHAKESPEARE
Medea, in E. *M.*, 29 ff., 35 ff., 135, 148
Medea, see EURIPIDES
MEILHAC-HALÉVY, *Froufrou*, 154
Menelaus, in E. *I. at A.*, 19
— in E. *Androm.*, 40
Merchant of Venice, The, see SHAKESPEARE
Mercutio, in Sh. *R. and J.*, 151; his Queen Mab speech, 156, 158
Merry Wives of Windsor, The, see SHAKESPEARE
Messengers in Greek tragedy, 156 n.
Micawber, 138
Michael and his Lost Angel, see JONES
Micio, in Terence, *Brothers*, 196
Midsummer Night's Dream, see SHAKESPEARE
Milestones, see BENNETT
Miranda, in Sh. *Tp.*, 156
Misalliance, see SHAW
Misanthrope, Le, see MOLIÈRE
MOLIÈRE, 121, 148–9
— *George Dandin*, 116 n.
— [*L'Avare*], 141–2
— *Le Misanthrope*, 150, 176, 197
— *Tartuffe*, 124, 184
M. Piégois, see CAPUS
MONTAGUE, MR. C. E., *Dramatic Values*, p. 27 qd., 116 n.; p. 227 qd., 156 n.; pp. 180 et seq. referred to, 180 n.
Montagues and Capulets, in Sh. *R. and J.*, 158
Morell, Rev. James, in Shaw, *Cand.*, 12–3, 16, 103–4
Mozart, 133
Mrs. Dane's Defence, 180
— *Gorringe's Necklace*, see DAVIES
— *Warren's Profession*, see SHAW
de Mullins, The Last of the, see HANKIN
DE MUSSET, 125

Nan, The Tragedy of, see MASEFIELD
Napoleon, 6, 134; in Shaw, *Man of D.,* 15–6
Nereus, mentioned in E. *I. at A.,* 19
Nora Helmer, in I. *D.'s H.,* 56, 131, 180, 194
Notorious Mrs. Ebbsmith, The, see PINERO
Nym, in Sh., 151

Oberon, in Sh. *M. N. Dr.,* 165
O'Connell, Amy, in B. *Waste,* 89, 95
Œdipus, in S. *Œ. Col.,* 171; in *Œ. Tyr.,* 179
Œdipus Coloneus, Rex, Tyrannus, see SOPHOCLES
Old Wives' Tale, see PEELE
Olivia, in Sh. *Tw. N.,* 200
One of the Best, 138
On ne badine pas avec l'amour, see DE MUSSET
Orestes, in Æ., 146–7; *Choeph.,* 190; in E. *El.,* 24–5, 27; *Or.,* 148
Orestes, see EURIPIDES
Orgon, in M. *Tartuffe,* 184
Othello, in Sh. *Oth.,* 167, 182, 185
Othello, see SHAKESPEARE
OTWAY, THOMAS, *Venice Preserv'd,* 180

Palmerston, 2
Paris, mentioned in E. *I. at A.,* 41
Patrick Cullen, Sir, in Shaw, *Dr.'s Dil.* (qd.), 9
Patterne, Sir Willoughby, 138
Paulina, in Sh. *A W.'s T.,* 200
Peace, The, see ARISTOPHANES
PEELE, GEORGE, *Old Wives' Tale,* 157
Peer Gynt, see IBSEN
Peleus, 19, 21
Pelias, 29
Pericles, 2
Persæ, see ÆSCHYLUS
Perseus, 137
Persians, in Æ. *Persæ,* 185
Peter Pan, see BARRIE

Phædra, in E. *Hippol.,* 148, 168
Phèdre, see RACINE
Philanderers, The, see SHAW
Philistines, The, see JONES
PHILLIPS, STEPHEN, 59
Phormio, see TERENCE
Pickwick, Samuel, 139
Piégois, M., see CAPUS
Pierre, in Otway, *V. Pres.,* 181
Pigeon, The, see GALSWORTHY
PINERO, SIR ARTHUR, 53, 55, 60, 68–70, 105, 173
Pistol, in Sh., 151
Plantagenet kings, in Sh., 140
— mother in Robertson, *Caste,* 62
Plato and women, 34
Playboy of the Western World, see SYNGE
Players, in Sh. *Hamlet,* 142
Playmaking, see ARCHER
Plutus, see ARISTOPHANES
Pogram, Elijah, in Dickens, *M. Chuz.,* 203
Polonius, in Sh. *H.,* 115 n., 143–4
Polydorus, in E. *Hecuba,* 169
Polyxena, in E. *Hecuba,* 169
Pompey the Great, see MASEFIELD
Portia, in Sh. *M. of V.,* 140, 154, 168, 202
Preserving Mr. Panmure, see PINERO
Prince Hal, in Sh. *Hy. IV.,* 168
Prism, Miss, in W. *Import.,* 200
Private Secretary, The, 12
PROFESSOR A. C. BRADLEY, *Shakespearean Tragedy,* 115 n., 142–3
Professor of Greek, in Shaw, *Maj. B.,* 7
Prometheus, in Æ. *Prom. V.,* 147, 169
Prometheus Bound, see ÆSCHYLUS
— *Unbound,* see SHELLEY
— *Vinctus,* see ÆSCHYLUS
Prospero, in Sh. *Tp.,* 128 and n., 141, 165, 203; his narrative, 156

INDEX OF PERSONS AND WORKS 219

Prunella, see BARKER and HOUSMAN
Puck, in Sh. *M. N. Dr.*, 165
Punch, 3, 53
Pygmalion, see SHAW
Pylades, 170

RACINE, *Phèdre*, 156 n.
Raina, in Shaw, *A. and M.*, 150, 169
Ramsden, in Shaw, *Man and Sup.*, 176
Raphael's " School of Athens," 129
" Récits de Théramène," 156 n.
Réjane, Mme., 192
Renault, in Otway, *V. Pres.*, 181
Return of the Native, The, see HARDY
Return of the Prodigal, The, see HANKIN
Rhesus, see EURIPIDES
ROBERTSON, THOMAS, 49–50, 53, 61–2, 66, 107
— — *Caste*, 49, 53 ; characters in, 62
Robinson Crusoe, 107
Robinson Crusoe, see DEFOE
ROCHEFOUCAULD, LA, see LA R.
Rodin, 73
Roman triumvirs, in Sh., 140
Romeo, in Sh. *R. and J.*, 128, 158, 171, 175
Romeo and Juliet, see SHAKESPEARE
Rosalind, in Sh. *As You*, 141
Rosmersholm, see IBSEN
ROSTAND, M., *Chantecler*, 153, 156, 163

Sabine, in Hervieu, *La C. du F.*, 151, 176
Sabine Women, The, see ANDREIEV
Saranoff, in Shaw, *A. and M.*, 12, 16 ff., 169
Sartorius, Blanche, in Shaw, *Wid. Ho.*, 101
SCHILLER, 48
SCHNITZLER, *Anatol*, 174

School for Scandal, screen-scene in, see SHERIDAN
" School of Athens," 129
SCOTT, SIR WALTER, 49
Second Mrs. Tanqueray, The see PINERO
SHAKESPEARE, 52, 69, 84, 101, 115 n., 140, 142 ff., 148, 158, 182, 187–8, 198 ; as comedian, 121 ; his chief aim, 54, 124
— *Antony and Cleopatra*, 136
— *As You Like It*, 170
— *Coriolanus*, hostile collision in, 150
— *Cymbeline* (qd.), weak conclusion of, 169, 198, 203
— *Hamlet*, 112 n., 122, 142 ff. ; ERVINE on, and peripeteia in, 115 n. ; supernatural agency in, 165
— *Henry the Fifth*, 138, 156, 175
— *Henry the Fourth*, 150, 168, 203
— *Henry the Sixth*, a chronicle, 140
— *Julius Cæsar*, 133, 135–6 (qd.), 196–7 ; funeral speech in, 156 ; catastrophe in, 181–2
— *King Lear*, 151
— *Macbeth*, 53, 112, 167, 175, 188–9 ; double recoil in, 178
— *Measure for Measure*, 200
— *Merchant of Venice*, 75–6 (qd.), 150, 165, 170 ; preparation for peripeteia in, 187 ; Fifth Act, peripeteia, *dénouement*, and conclusion in, 201
— *Merry Wives of Windsor*, 138
— *Midsummer Night's Dream*, 203 ; magic in, 165
— *Othello*, 117 ff. ; a melodrama, 124, 137, 150, 167 ; catastrophe of, 185
— *Romeo and Juliet*, 128, 172, 175 ; accident in, 151 ; Mab speech in, 156–7

SHAKESPEARE, *Tempest*, 127, 128 n.; accident in, 130, 151; magic in, 165; Prospero's narrative in, 156, 203
— *Titus Andronicus*, 133
— *Twelfth Night*, 108, 200
— *Winter's Tale, The*, 165, 200
Shakespearean Tragedy, see BRADLEY
SHAW, MR. GEORGE BERNARD, 1-48 *passim*, 52, 58, 60, 71, 74, 79 ff., 95 ff., 155, 173
— — *Androcles and the Lion*, 100
— — *Arms and the Man*, 12, 150, 169
— — *Back to Methuselah*, 98-9
— — *Blanco Posnet*, 99
— — *Cæsar and Cleopatra* (qd.), 42 ff., 97-8
— — *Candida*, 10, 12 ff., 103 (qd.)
— — *Captain Brassbound's Conversion*, 22-3
— — *Devil's Disciple*, 14-5, 96 ff.
— — *Doctor's Dilemma*, 8
— — *Don Juan in Hell* = Act iii. of *Man and Sup.*, 102
— — *Getting Married*, 101, 174, 186
— — *Heartbreak House*, 98, 193
— — *How He Lied to her Husband*, 9
— — *John Bull's Other Island*, 32, 104
— — *Major Barbara*, 7, 32, 43-4, 99, 101, 179; dialogue in, 159
— — *Man and Superman*, 39, 150, 176, 196
— — *Man of Destiny*, 15-6
— — *Mrs. Warren's Profession*, 32, 39, 122
— — *Pygmalion*, 160
— — *The Philanderers*, 101
— — *Widowers' Houses*, 32
— — *You Never Can Tell*, 101
SHELLEY, 4
— *Prometheus Unbound*, 147

Sheraton, 106
SHERIDAN, 50; *Critic*, 49-50; *School for Scandal*, 185
Shylock, in Sh. *M. of V.*, 75-6, 139, 168, 182, 187-8 (qd.), 201-2
Silver Box, The, see GALSWORTHY
Skin Game, The, see GALSWORTHY
Smith, Sydney, 4
Solness and others, in I. *M. B.*, 136
SOPHOCLES, 54, 115 n., 121, 125, 146, 148, 172; dialogue in, 155; his chief aim, 54, 124
— *Ajax*, 171, 209
— *Antigone*, 149-50, 170
— *Œdipus Coloneus*, 122, 171
— *Œdipus Rex* (=*Tyr.*), 53
— *Œdipus Tyrannus*, 123, 124, 163, 196; accident in, 127-8; complication, peripeteia, solution in, 178
— *Philoctetes*, 154
Spanish Tragedy, see KYD
Sphinx, in Shaw, *C. and Cl.*, 42
Spintho, in Shaw, *Andro.*, 100
Stangy, in Hervieu, *La C. du F.*, 176
Stephano, in Sh. *Tp.*, 202
STEPHEN PHILLIPS, 59
Stockmann, in I. *En. Peo.*, 57 (qd.), 172
Strife, see GALSWORTHY, 57
Supplices, see ÆSCHYLUS
SUTRO, MR. ALFRED, 66-7
Swindon, Major, in Shaw, *Devil's D.*, 15
SYNGE, J. M., dialogue in, 155; *The Playboy of the Western World*, peripeteia in, 185

Talbot, in Sh. [*Hy. VI.*], 140
Tanner, John, in Shaw, *Man and Sup.*, 150, 176, 196
Tanqueray, Mrs., in P. *Second Mrs. T.*, 69-70
Tartuffe, in M. *Tart.*, 184
Tartuffe, see MOLIÈRE
TCHEKOF, 98, 192

INDEX OF PERSONS AND WORKS 221

Tempest, The, see SHAKESPEARE
TENNYSON, 3–4, 59
TERENCE, 185; dramaturgic economy of, 169; *Phormio,* 185; *The Brothers,* 185; climax in, 196
Tess of the D'Urbervilles, see HARDY
Teucer, in S. *Ajax,* 171
THACKERAY, 49
"Théramène, Récits de," 156 n.
Thetis, 17, 19
Tims, in G. *Pigeon,* 81
Title, The, see BENNETT
Titus Andronicus, see SHAKESPEARE
Tortoise, in Rostand, *Chantecler,* 153
Tragedy of Nan, see MASEFIELD
Trebell, Henry, in B. *Waste,* 52, 89, 94 ff.
Trench, Harry, in Shaw, *Wid. Ho.,* 101
Trenchard, Voysey, in B. *V. Inherit.,* 92
Trinculo, in Sh. *Tp.,* 202
Trois Filles de M. Dupont, Les, see BRIEUX
Trojans, in E. *I. at A.,* 41; *Rhesus,* 194; in Homer, 18
Tubal, in Sh. *M. of V.,* 170
Tudor nobles, in Sh., 140
Twelfth Night, see SHAKESPEARE
Two Mr. Wetherbys, The, see HANKIN
Tybalt, in Sh. *R. and J.,* 151, 175
Types of Tragic Drama, see VAUGHAN

"Uncle Peter," as *deus ex machina,* 164, 176
Undershaft, in Shaw, *Maj. B.* (qd.), 43–4
— Barbara, in Shaw, *Maj. B.,* 179
— Stephen, in Shaw, *Maj. B.* (qd.), 43–4

Valentine, in Shaw, *You Never,* 101
VANBRUGH, 50
VAUGHAN, PROFESSOR C. E., *Types of Tragic Drama,* 115 n.
Venice Preserv'd, see OTWAY
Victoria, Queen, 5
Viola, in Sh. *Tw. N.,* 200
Viveurs, see LAVEDAN
Voysey family, in B. *V. Inherit.,* 88, 91, 93–4, 195
Voysey Inheritance, The, see BARKER

WALKLEY, MR. A. B., *Drama and Life,* 142 ff., 160 and n.
— — *Professor Bradley's "Hamlet,"* 143–4 (qd.)
— — on Sh. *Hamlet,* 157 n.
Walpole, Horace, his saying on life, 117
— Sir Robert, and stage censorship, 49
Waste, see BARKER
Watchman, in S. *Antigone,* 170
Watts, the painter, 72
WELLS, MR. H. G., *Love and Mr. Lewisham,* 92
Werle, Gregers, in I. *Wild Duck,* 76
Wetherby, Richard, in H. *The Two Mr. W.'s,* 199–200
Wetherbys, The Two Mr., see HANKIN
Whitefield, Ann, in Shaw, *Man and Sup.,* 150, 196
Widowers' Houses, see SHAW
Wild Duck, in I. *W. D.,* 206
Wild Duck, The, see IBSEN
WILDE, OSCAR, 60 ff., **66, 75,** 79, 103, 105, 180 and n.
— — dialogue in, 161–2
— — *Lady Windermere's Fan,* 61; catastrophe and dénouement in, 180
— — *The Importance of Being Earnest,* 12, 60, 119
Windermere, Lady, in W. *Ly. W.'s Fan,* 180

Windermere, Lord, in W. *Ly. W.'s Fan*, 180
Winter's Tale, The, see SHAKESPEARE
WORDSWORTH, 3

Yorick, in Sh. *Hamlet*, 142
You Never Can Tell, see SHAW

Zeus, in Æ. *Prom. V.*, 169, 207

GENERAL INDEX

Accident in drama, 126 ff.
Action, Unity of, 208
Æschylean plays, 202; scenes in Goethe's *Faust*, 147; trilogy, 202
Aim of art, 125–6; of dramatic art, 123 ff.; of Ibsen, Shakespeare, and Sophocles, 54, 124
Amateur productions, 108
Americans, 4, 194
Anglo-Indian Colonel, in H. *Charity*, 78
Apron-stage of Elizabethan theatre, 157
Architectonic skill, necessary in drama, 50; of Ibsen, 57
Art and Science, 72
Art, object of, 124
Athenian citizen, in Ar. *Acharnians*, 183
— decadence, 6; democracy, 57; dramatists, 57; literature, 6; ochlocracy, 57; patriotism, 6; philosophy, 6; politics, 6; women, 33
Audience, Elizabethan, 181; English, 181

Bow of Philoctetes, in S. *Philoc.*, 154
Burlesque, 121
"Bushiness," in drama, esp. Russian d., 192–3
"Business," 153–4

Canon, in W. *Import.*, 200
Carpets, in Æ. *Agam.*, 154
Caskets, in Sh. *M. of V.*, 154
Catastrophe, 175, 196; in tragedy, 185; liable to a special danger, 191 ff.; misuse of the word, 206; not "disaster," 206
Catastrophe, in I. *A D.'s Ho.*, 179–80
— in W. *Ly. W.'s Fan*, 180
— in Sh. *Macb.*, 179
— in S. *Œ. Tyr.*, 179
— in Sh. *Oth.*, 185
— in M. *Tartuffe*, 184
— in Terence, *The Brothers*, 185
Censorship Commission, 95
— of stage, 49, 56
Character-drawing of Ibsen, 56
Characterisation in drama, 132 ff.
"Circumstance" in tragedy, 206
Classical and romantic drama, 170
— dialogue in Ibsen, 172–3
"Click," in drama, 151 ff.
Climax, 196, 206
Coincidence in drama, 127
Collision in drama, 145 n., 150–1
Comedy, 117, 145
— of Manners, 60 ff., 148
— peripeteia in, 177
— Roman, 123
— what it is, 116 ff.
Complication in drama, 193; in life, 111
— in S. *Œ. Tyr.*, 178
— liable to a special danger, 191
Conclusion in drama, 196
Contrast in drama, 145 n.
Conventions in drama, 118
Crisis in drama, 145 n., 175

GENERAL INDEX

Crutch, in I. *Little Eyolf*, 154
"Curtain," 152
— "descends on a note of interrogation," 193
— "effective," 63; "strong," 204

Danger of prose-dialogue, 159
Dangers of catastrophe, complication, *dénouement*, 191
— of various dramatic dialogue-forms, 156 ff.
Dark Age of English dramatic literature (1779–1889), 49
Death of hero not a necessary ingredient in tragedy, 122
Debate in B.'s plays, 94
Delian League, 6
Delphic Oracle, in E. *El.*, 24, 45; in Sh. *The W.'s T.*, 165
Dénouement, 114, 163, 175, 176, 196, 197, 206
— danger to which it is liable, 191
— in Ar. *Acharn.*, 183
— in E. *Alc.*, 130
— in I. *AD.'s Ho.*, 180, 194
— in Otway, *Ven. Pres.*, 180–1
— in Sh. *J. C.*, 182, 197
— in Sh. *M. of V.*, 201
— in S. *Œ. Tyr.*, 178
— in W. *Ly. W.'s Fan*, 180
— weaknesses in, 193 ff.
— whence it should arise, 132
Desis, of Aristotle, 132
Deus ex machina, "Uncle Peter" as, 164 ff., 191
Dialogue, Economy in, 170 ff.
— in Congreve, 150; in Hankin, 79; in Ibsen, 162, 172–3; in Maeterlinck, 155; in Molière, 148; in Rostand, 155; in Shaw, 155; in Sophocles, 155; in Synge, 155, 185; in Wilde, 161–2
— poetical form or prose form, 155
— varieties of, in drama, 154 ff.
Didacticism in drama, 125–6
Difficulty appropriately solved, in every play, 111

Double recoil, in Sh. *Macb.*, 178
Drama of types, 149–50
— Russian, 192
"Drama," The word, 110
Drama, what it is, 111
Dramatic art, Forms or types of, 115 ff.
— — its aim, 125
— collision, 150
— conventions as they affect the four types, 118–9
— intensity, 152
— manner, 144
"Dramatic," The word, 145; wrong use of, 204–5
Dramatic types, Occasional approximation of, to each other, 116–7
Duke (Orsino), in Sh. *Tw. N.*, 200
— (Vincentio), in Sh. *M. for M.*, 200

Economy in dialogue, 170 ff.
— in drama, 163
— in management of character, 166 ff.
— in solution, 166 f.
Education Act, 1870, 2
Elizabethan audiences, 181; plays, 200; theatre, 157
Entertainment by drama, 80, 124 ff.
— common aim of all dramas, 124
Exhibition, The Great (1851), 3
Explanatory domestics, 135
External events or happenings, in drama, 126 ff.

"Falling over," 175
Farce, 116 ff., 128, 152; deals with experiences of particular persons, 119; good, 118; horseplay in, 118; how it differs from comedy, 119; what it is, 116 ff.
Fate in tragedy, 206–7
— puppets of, 206–7
Fool, in Sh. *Lear*, 151

French, The, 4
— critics, 53; farces, 108; tragedy and the Three Unities, 208; tragic playwrights, 121; windows in modern drama, 162, 204
Fundamental characteristics of E. and Shaw, 7 ff.
Funeral speech, in Sh. *J. C.*, 156; is the peripeteia, 182

Greek comedy and tragedy parts of religious ritual, 123
— spirit of inquiry, 10
Greeks, 16 ff., 20
Greek theatre, 157

Handkerchief, in Sh. *Oth.*, 154
"Happy ending," 56, 77–8, 199
Hebrews, 75
Hero, Conventional stage, and Shaw, 16
Horseplay in farce, 118
Hostile collision in drama, 150
"Huddled ending," *e.g.* in Sh. *Cymb.*, 198
Humours, Drama of, 149

Ibsenism, 64, 105
Ibsenists, English, 71, 76, 105–6
Intensity in drama, 152
Interaction of characters in drama, 114
Interpretation of life the task of a dramatist, 207–8
Irishman, The comic, 65
Irrational elements in drama, Aristotle on these, 130

"Knot, Untying of the," 114

Lady, The, in Shaw, *M. of D.*, 15
Life-force, in Shaw, 102
"London successes," 108

Magic in drama, 165
"Main plot," 202
Mannequin - scene in B. *Madras H.*, 154

Manners, Comedy of, 60 ff., 149
Material details, Use of, in projecting character, 133 f.
Mediæval plays, 123
Melodrama, 118, 128, 133, 152; and Shaw, 13; good, E.'s *Helena* one, 119; how distinguished from tragedy, 119; *Othello* a (?), 117; physical action in, 120; spectacular element in, 120; theatricality in, 119; violence in, 120; what it is, 116 ff.
Messengers' speeches in Greek tragedy, 156 n.
Methods of drama, 126 ff.
"Middle" of a play, 174 ff.
Miracle-play, 112
Misuse of various words, 203 ff.
Mohammedanism in B. *Madras H.*, 91
Morality, in I. and Shaw, 58–9
Morality plays, 147
Muffins, in W. *Import.*, 119

National theatre, 86
Neo-British School, 62, 63, 66 ff., 69, 77
Nurse, in Sh. *R. and J.*, 171

Object of art, 124
Olympian gods, 10
— religion, 25
Opera, 121
Oracle, Delphic, 24, 45, 165
"Overthrow," 175; in Shaw, *Maj. B.*, 179

Pantomimes, 121
Particular and universal in drama, 146 ff.
Peloponnesian War, 6
Peripeteia, 175 ff., 196, 206
— in Æ. *Persæ*, 185–6; *Prom. V.*, 177
— in Ar. *Ach.*, 183; *Birds*, 184; *Frogs*, 177, 184; *Peace*, 184; *Plutus*, 183
— in Bennett, *Honeymoon*, 197
— in I. *D.'s Ho.*, 179
— in H. A. Jones, *Mrs. Dane's Defence*, 180

GENERAL INDEX

Peripeteia in M. *Misanthrope*, 197; *Tartuffe*, 184
— in Otway, *Ven. Pres.*, 180
— in Sh. *Hamlet*, 115 n.; *J. C.*, 181–2; *Macb.*, 178; *M. of V.*, 201; *Oth.*, 185
— in Shaw, *Maj. B.*, 179
— in Sheridan, *School for Sc.*, 185
— in S. *Œ. Tyr.*, 178
— in Synge, *Playboy*, 185
— in Terence, *Brothers*, 184–5
— in Wilde, *Ly. W.'s Fan*, 180
— in comedy, 177, 182–3; in every drama, 186; its three qualities, 177; preparation for, 186 ff.; where does it occur? 177
Philistines, and their watchword, 126
Physical action in melodrama, 120
Place, Unity of, 208–9
Plot, 111 ff.; an organism, 113–4; how is it worked? 174 ff.; the " soul of the play," 144; the *unum necessarium* in drama, 113
Poetic dialogue, 155
" Poetical drama," 59
Post-Ibsenist manner, 71
Postman, in modern drama, 63
Poverty, in Shaw, 32
Pre-Ibsenists, 104
Preparation for the peripeteia, 186 ff.; in Sh. *Macb.*, 188; *M. of V.*, 187–8
Probability, 166
" Problem-play," 65
Projection of a character, 133 ff.
Propagandist playwrights, 126
Prose dialogue, 155; rule for, 160
Pseudo-Ibsenism, 66; Ibsenist school, 64
Psychological trend of modern English dramatic criticism, 115 and n.
Psychology in drama, 131 ff.
" Puppets of Fate," 206

Question - and - answer plot, 123

Question of a drama, whence it should arise, 132
— of the play, 177

Realism and reality, 71 ff.
Recitations on the stage, 157–8
" Récits de Théramène," 156 n.
" Recoil," 175; double r., or repeated r., in Sh. *Macb.*, 178
— in Ar., 183; in M. *Tart.*, 184; in Shaw, *Maj. B.*, 179; and see Peripeteia
" Reinforced reminiscence," 125
Renaissance of English Drama, The Present, 49–108
Repertory theatres, 107–8
Revenge, in E. and Shaw, 22
" Reversal," 175; in Shaw, *Maj. B.*, 179; and see Peripeteia
Revues, 121
Roman comedy and tragedy, 123
Russian drama, " bushiness " in, 192
— influence on English drama, 193
— playwrights, 192

Saint Crispin's Day harangue, in Sh. *Hy. V.*, 175
Salvation Army, in Shaw, *Maj. B.*, 179
Science and art, 72
Screen-scene, in Sheridan, *Sch. for Sc.*, 185
Semi-Ibsenist, 71
Sexes, Relations of the, in E. and Shaw, 31
Simplicity not the same thing as economy, in drama, 163
Situations, in Ibsen, 56
Slaves, in Aristotle, and E., 33
" Slice of life," 149, 207–8
Social inequality, in E., 32 ff.
Solonian régime, 33
Solution, in drama, 114, 124, 193, 196; in I. *D.'s Ho.*, 179–80; in S. *Œ. Tyr.*, 178–9

Sophists, 6
Spartan confederacy, in Ar. *Ach.*, 183
Staginess, 52
"Strong curtains," 204; "strong scene," 70
Supernatural in drama, 165
Surprise in drama, 166

Theatricality and drama not the same, 110
— in melodrama, 119
— in modern drama, 204
Three Unities, 208-9
Time, Unity of, 208
Tortoise, in Rostand, *Chantecler*, 153
Tragedy, 118, 145, 205; misuse of the word, 205; peripeteia in, 177; Roman, 123; what it is, 116 ff.
Tragi-comedy, a " mechanical mixture," 117
Transcendentalists, 73-4

" Truth to life," 159
" Tying," in drama, 132
Types, Jonson a dramatist of, 148-9

" Uncle Peter" as *deus ex machina*, 164, 191
Underplot, 202; in I., 57
Unities, The Three, 208-9
Universal and particular in drama, 146 ff.
" Untying of the knot," 114, 163

Victorian age, 2 ff.
Violence, in melodrama, 120

Watchman, in S. *Antigone*, 170
Waterloo, Battle of, 181
" Weltvernichtungsidee," 183
Wit, of E. and Shaw, 40
Women, in B., 90 ff. ; in E., 33 ff. ; in Plato, 34; in Shaw, 31 ff.

For Product Safety Concerns and Information please contact our EU
representative GPSR@taylorandfrancis.com
Taylor & Francis Verlag GmbH, Kaufingerstraße 24, 80331 München, Germany

www.ingramcontent.com/pod-product-compliance
Lightning Source LLC
Chambersburg PA
CBHW062217300426
44115CB00012BA/2097